TO LOVE AND TO CHERISH

A Wedding with a Difference

Oliver Brennan

First published 2006 by
Veritas Publications
7/8 Lower Abbey Street
Dublin 1, Ireland
Email publications@veritas.ie
Website www.veritas.ie

10 9 8 7 6 5 4 3 2 1

ISBN 1-85390-827-4
ISBN 978-1-85390-827-9

Cover design by Niamh McGarry
Printed in the Republic of Ireland by Betaprint, Dublin

Veritas books are printed on paper made from the wood pulp of managed forests. For every tree felled, at least one tree is planted, thereby renewing natural resources.

CONTENTS

INTRODUCTION

We live in an age that is becoming increasingly open to the spiritual dimension of human existence. More and more couples whom I accompany in preparation for their marriage say that the most important part of their wedding day is what happens in the church. This is equally true of those who are not regular church-goers as it is of those who participate in the celebration of the Eucharist each weekend. Your desire to be married in a church shows that there is something 'sacred' about your love. Your relationship embodies something special that transcends the realm of a mundane experience.

This book is a response to the myriad requests I receive for help in the preparation of the marriage ceremony. Its purpose is to offer a choice among the rich variety of readings, prayers, reflections, forms of exchanging the marriage vows, blessing of rings, prayers of the faithful, marriage prefaces and nuptial blessings that are available.

When real friendship and deep love awaken in your life it leads to a re-birth of the human heart. Each couple approaching marriage is a unique pair, carrying in their hearts a love that is overflowing and generous. It is important, then, that they have the opportunity to choose from among the words, music and song what is most appropriate to their life experience. This will ensure that the wedding liturgy is the most significant aspect of the day and sets the tone for the remainder of the great celebration. It would be hoped that through careful preparation the wedding ceremony will touch the hearts of the bride and groom, as well as the whole wedding party, in a deeply human and spiritual way.

For most people, being involved in planning a significant liturgy is a whole new experience. It is a privilege and a good pastoral opportunity to work with a couple at this moment in their lives. The meaningfulness or otherwise of the marriage ceremony can be determinative of the future relationship they will have with the faith community into which they were initiated as children.

The Constitution on the Liturgy of the Second Vatican Council reminds us that the sacraments 'not only pre-suppose faith, but by words and objects they also nourish, strengthen and express it ... It is therefore of capital importance that the faithful easily understand the sacramental signs' (n. 59). The preparation for and celebration of a wedding liturgy provides a golden opportunity to effect this. The marriage liturgy is one of the most important religious experiences for people during their adult lives.

Few, if any, events in life surpass that of the celebration of marriage. The occasion of a marriage is one of extraordinary joy, excitement and happiness, not only for the couple, but also for their parents, grandparents, family members, bridal party and friends who gather to share in their promise of life-long faithful love in the Sacrament of Marriage.

The celebration of a marriage ceremony reminds us of a great truth of the human journey: the best things in life are free. This may seem a strange statement to those who are paying for the reception! Nevertheless, when we stop to think about what is really important in life, we recognise that the greatest gift that we can give to one another is the gift of our friendship, and even more especially our unconditional love. People gather to celebrate a wedding liturgy because a couple have gifted each other with unconditional friendship and love. A wedding ceremony touches the secret heart of life and brings what is best in life and experience to expression.

If we attend to the rhythm of nature we experience the spring season, as we may the dawn of each day, as a refreshing time, a time of possibility and promise. Entering into marriage is a new dawn, a new springtime in our lives, an occasion of great possibility and promise. The existential philosopher, Sören Kierkegaard, said something very profound about living when he wrote: 'If I could wish for something, I would wish for neither wealth nor power but the passion for possibility. I would wish only for an eye, which eternally young, eternally burns with the longing to see possibility.'

A wedding celebration is a time of endless possibility, especially the possibility of a life lived in utter fullness, a relationship which is mutually life-giving to each partner and to the wider community, particularly the community of faith of which the couple are a part. We are on this earth to live life to the full and when we are generous in our love, care and compassion somehow life comes to bless us.

MARRIAGE AS SACRAMENT

God's love is very concrete. It is experienced in a very particular way in human love, especially in the love relationship of marriage. There is a sense in which genuine love is beyond what words can say. A couple's love for each other is the embodiment of God's love. In other words, married love is an outward sign, a concrete image of God's love: this is why the Church uses the word 'sacrament' in relation to marriage. The ebb and flow of the divine–human relationship is most deeply reflected in the human love relationship, especially the marriage bond. God reaches out and touches us through the love of others and Christians believe that the risen Jesus is at the heart of all love. There is nothing magical or esoteric about the word 'sacrament'. It is really a way of naming a divine–human reality in religious language. The giving and receiving of human love is in essence the giving and receiving of God's love. This is what we mean when we say that the couple being married confer the sacrament on each other, or celebrate their unconditional love promise as sacrament. This is the nature of the love that is celebrated in the marriage ceremony. The couple's natural love is graced in a new way. Their relationship is enhanced through the sacramental presence of the risen Lord for the duration of their human journey.

SECTION I

WEDDING SERVICE

There are two ways of celebrating the wedding liturgy in a Catholic Church:

- A wedding service with Nuptial Mass;
- A wedding service without Mass.

This applies to mixed marriages (i.e. marriages between a Catholic and a non-Catholic) as well as to marriages between two Catholics. Before offering all the choices regarding the marriage rite, readings and prayers, I will give a complete sample of the wedding ceremony in the context of the celebration of the Eucharist and also a sample of the wedding service without Mass. On the basis of these two model wedding liturgies, a couple, with the help of the priest or minister, can choose from among the various options which follow and thereby personalise their wedding liturgy.

NUPTIAL MASS INCORPORATING THE RITE OF MARRIAGE

Introductory Rites

Entrance Music and/or Hymn

After the priest/minister personally greets the couple, he invites them to each light a single candle symbolising their coming to the church as single people OR the mothers of the bride and groom each light a candle as a symbol of the gift of their daughter and son to one another.

C.[1]   In the name of the Father and of the Son and of the Holy Spirit.

P.[2]   Amen.

C.   The grace and peace of God our Father and the Lord Jesus Christ be with you.

P.   And also with you.

Penitential Rite

C.   As we gather to celebrate God's sealing of N. and N.'s love we turn to our God of love with trust and confidence.
You are love itself:
Lord have mercy.

P.   Lord have mercy.

C.   You call us to imitate your love:
Christ have mercy.

P.   Christ have mercy.

C.   Sometimes we fail in this calling:
Lord have mercy.

1. Celebrant
2. People

P.   Lord have mercy.

C.   May almighty God have mercy on us, forgive us our sins
        and bring us to everlasting life.

P.   Amen.

Gloria

Glory to God in the highest,
and peace to his people on earth.
Lord God, heavenly King,
Almighty God and Father.
We worship you, we give you thanks, we praise you for your glory.
Lord Jesus Christ, only Son of the Father,
Lord God, Lamb of God,
you take away the sins of the world:
Have mercy on us.
You are seated at the right hand of the Father:
Receive our prayer.
For you alone are the Holy One.
You alone are the Lord.
You alone are the Most High,
Jesus Christ,
With the Holy Spirit,
In the glory of God the Father. Amen

Opening Prayer

C.   Let us pray.
        Father, hear our prayers for N. and N., who today are united in
        marriage before your altar. Give them your blessing and
        strengthen their love for each other.
        We ask this through our Lord Jesus Christ, your Son, who
        lives and reigns with you and the Holy Spirit, one God, for
        ever and ever.

P.   Amen.

Liturgy of the Word

First Reading

R.[3]   *A reading from the book of Ecclesiasticus (6:14-17)*
A faithful friend is a sure shelter. Whoever finds one has found a rare treasure. A faithful friend is something beyond price. There is no measuring their worth. A faithful friend is the elixir of life and those who love the Lord will find one. Whoever loves the Lord makes true friends, for as a person is, so is their friend.

This is the word of the Lord.

P.   Thanks be to God.

Psalm (Sung)

Psalm 148 (if recited)
Response: Praise the name of the Lord

Praise the Lord from the heavens,
praise him in the heights.
Praise him, all his angels,
praise him, all his host!   *Response*

Praise him, sun and moon,
praise him, shining stars.
Praise him, highest heavens
and the waters above the heavens   *Response*

3. Reader

All mountains and hills
all fruit trees and cedars,
beasts, wild and tame,
reptiles and birds on the wing. *Response*

All earth's kings and peoples,
earth's princes and rulers;
young men and maidens,
old men together with children. *Response*

Let them praise the name of the Lord
for he alone is exalted.
The splendour of his name
reaches beyond heaven and earth. *Response*

Second Reading

R.   *A reading from the first letter of St John (4:7-12)*
Beloved, let us love one another, because love is from God;
everyone who loves is born of God and knows God. Whoever
does not love does not know God, for God is love. God's love
was revealed among us in this way: God sent his only Son
into the world so that we might live through him. In this is
love, not that we loved God but that he loved us and sent his
Son to be the atoning sacrifice for our sins. Beloved, since
God loved us so much, we also ought to love one another. No
one has ever seen God; if we love one another, God lives in
us and his love is perfected in us.

This is the word of the Lord.

P.   Thanks be to God.

Gospel Acclamation

Alleluia Alleluia
As long as we love one another
God will live in us
And his love will be complete in us.
Alleluia.   *(1 John 4:12)*

Gospel

C.   The Lord be with you.

P.   And also with you.

C.   A reading from the holy Gospel according to John (15:9-11).

P.   Glory to you, O Lord.

C.   As the Father has loved me, so have I loved you: abide in my
      love. If you keep my commandments you will abide in my love,
      just as I have kept my Father's commandments and abide in his
      love. I have said these things to you so that my joy may be in
      you, and that your joy may be complete. This is my command-
      ment: that you love one another as I have loved you.

      This is the Gospel of the Lord.

P.   Praise to you Lord Jesus Christ.

Homily

Rite of Marriage

C.   Dear Children of God,

      You have come here today to pledge your love before God and
      before the Church here present in the person of the priest,
      your families and friends.

          In becoming husband and wife you give yourselves to each
      other for life. You promise to be true and faithful, to support
      and cherish each other all the days of your lives, so that your

years together will be the living out in love of the pledge you now make.

May your love for each other reflect the enduring love of Christ for his Church. As you face the future together, keep in mind that the sacrament of marriage unites you with Christ and brings you, through the years, the grace and blessing of God our Father. Marriage is from God: he alone can give you the happiness that goes beyond human expectation and that grows deeper through the difficulties and struggles of life. Put your trust in God as you set out together in life.

Make your home a centre of Christian family life. The Christian home makes Christ and his Church present in the world of everyday things. May all who enter your home find there the presence of the Lord for he has said, 'Where two or three are gathered together in my name, there am I in the midst of them'.

Now as you are about to exchange your marriage vows the Church wishes to be assured that you appreciate the meaning of what you do, and so I ask you: have you come here of your own free will and choice to marry each other?

Both   We have.

C.   Will you love and cherish each other in marriage all the days of your life?

Both   We will.

C.   Are you willing to accept with love the children God may send you and bring them up in accordance with the law of Christ and his Church?

Both   We are.

Declaration of Consent

C.   I invite you to declare before God and his Church your consent to become husband and wife.

Bride (B.) and groom (G.) join hands:

G.   I, N., take you N. as my wife,
For better, for worse,
For richer, for poorer,
In sickness and in health.
I will love and cherish you all the days of my life.

B.   I, N., take you N. as my husband,
For better, for worse,
For richer, for poorer,
In sickness and in health.
I will love and cherish you all the days of my life.

C.   What God joins together, no one should separate. May the Lord confirm the consent that you have given and enrich you with his blessing.

P.   Amen.

Blessing of Rings

C.   Almighty God, bless these rings, symbols of faithfulness and unbroken love. May N. and N. always be true to each other. May they be one in heart and mind. May they be united in love forever.
Through Christ our Lord.

P.   Amen.

Exchange of Rings

The groom places the ring on the bride's finger saying:

G.   N., wear this ring as a sign of my friendship and faithful love. In the name of the Father and of the Son and of the Holy Spirit. Amen.

The bride places the ring on the groom's finger saying:

B.   N., wear this ring as a sign of my friendship and faithful love. In the name of the Father and of the Son and of the Holy Spirit. Amen.

The bride and groom may exchange gifts as a sign that from this day forward they share everything.

G.   N., I give you this gift as a token of all I possess.
B.   N., I give you this gift as a token of all I possess.

Lighting of the Marriage Candle
Together the bride and groom light a single candle from the two candles they (or their mothers) lit at the beginning of the Mass as a symbol of their union as husband and wife.

Prayer of the Newly Married Couple (Optional)
We thank you Lord,
and we praise you
for bringing us
to this happy day.
You have given us to each other.
Now, together, we give ourselves to you.
We ask you, Lord:
make us one in our love.
Keep us one in your peace.
Protect our marriage.
Bless our home.
Make us gentle.
Keep us faithful.
And when life is over
unite us again
where parting is no more

in the kingdom of your love.
There we will praise you
in the happiness and peace
of our eternal home.
Amen.

Prayers of the Faithful

C.   God has given us the promise of fidelity and love in the Word of Scripture. N. and N. have given their promise of life-long faithful love in the Sacrament of Marriage. This hour of promise is also a time of prayer.
We turn to God with confidence.

R.   For N. and N., that the Lord who has brought them to this happy day will keep them forever in fidelity and love. May today's graced sacramental moment be always active in them.
Lord hear us.

P.   Lord graciously hear us.

R.   For our families, relatives and friends who walk with us on life's journey and especially for all who have helped N. and N. reach this happy day. May they continue to support them on their new journey, which begins at this altar.
Lord hear us.

P.   Lord graciously hear us.

R.   That all Church leaders may be blessed in their efforts to make faith relevant in the lives of people today.
Lord hear us.

P.   Lord graciously hear us.

R.   That all people in the world may experience justice and peace and especially that children may grow up in a peaceful and caring society.

Lord hear us.

P. Lord graciously hear us.

R. For all who nurture young people and act as God's co-creators in developing their talents, that the fruits of their work may bring variety, joy and inspiration to our lives.
Lord hear us.

P. Lord graciously hear us.

R. For all who have died, especially those whom we have known and loved, that they may enjoy perfect happiness and total fulfilment in eternal life.
Lord hear us.

P. Lord graciously hear us.

C. O ever-loving and caring God, as we celebrate this sacramental moment in the lives of N. and N., we pray that their love may continue to deepen as they journey through life together.
We ask this through Christ our Lord.

P. Amen.

Liturgy of the Eucharist

Preparation of the Gifts

C. Blessed are you Lord, God of all creation.
Through your goodness we have this bread to offer, which earth has given and human hands have made. It will become for us the bread of life.

P. Blessed be God for ever.

C. By the mystery of this water and wine may we come to share in the divinity of Christ who humbled himself to share in our humanity.
Blessed are you Lord, God of all creation.

Through your goodness we have this wine to offer, fruit of the vine and work of human hands. It will become our spiritual drink.

P. Blessed be God for ever.

C. Pray my sisters and brothers that our sacrifice may be acceptable to God, the almighty Father.

P. May the Lord accept the sacrifice at your hands, for the praise and glory of God's name, for our good and the good of all God's Church.

Prayer over the Gifts

C. Lord, accept our offering for N. and N. By your love and providence you have brought them together. Now bless them all the days of their married life.
We ask this through Christ our Lord.

P. Amen.

Eucharistic Prayer

C. The Lord be with you.

P. And also with you.

C. Lift up your hearts.

P. We lift them up to the Lord.

C. Let us give thanks to the Lord our God.

P. It is right to give him thanks and praise.

C. Father,
All-powerful and ever-living God, we do well always and everywhere to give you thanks. You created man and woman in love to share your divine life. We see their high destiny in the love of husband and wife, which bears the imprint of your own divine love. Love is man and woman's origin, love is their constant calling, love is their fulfilment in heaven. The love of man and woman is made holy in the sacrament of marriage and becomes the mirror of your everlasting love. Through Christ the choirs of angels and all the saints praise

and worship your glory. May our voices blend with theirs as we join in their unending hymn of praise:

P.   Holy, holy, holy Lord,
       God of power and might,
       heaven and earth are full of your glory.
       Hosanna in the highest.
       Blessed is he who comes in the name of the Lord.
       Hosanna in the highest.

C.   Father, you are holy indeed,
       And all creation rightly gives you praise.
       All life, all holiness comes from you through your Son, Jesus Christ our Lord, by the working of the Holy Spirit.
       From age to age you gather a people to yourself, so that from east to west a perfect offering may be made to the glory of your name. And so Father, we bring you these gifts.
       We ask you to make them holy by the power of your Spirit that they may become the body and blood of your Son, our Lord Jesus Christ, at whose command we celebrate this Eucharist.
       On the night he was betrayed he took the bread and gave you thanks and praise.
       He broke the bread, gave it to his disciples and said:
       TAKE THIS, ALL OF YOU, AND EAT IT.
       THIS IS MY BODY, WHICH WILL BE GIVEN UP FOR YOU.
       When supper was ended he took the cup. Again he gave you thanks and praise, gave the cup to his disciples and said:
       TAKE THIS, ALL OF YOU, AND DRINK FROM IT.
       THIS IS THE CUP OF MY BLOOD,
       THE BLOOD OF THE NEW AND EVERLASTING COVENANT.
       IT WILL BE SHED FOR YOU AND FOR ALL
       SO THAT SINS MAY BE FORGIVEN.
       DO THIS IN MEMORY OF ME.

       Let us proclaim the mystery of faith.

Memorial Acclamation of the People

P.   *Response (sung)*

C.   Father,

Calling to mind the death your Son endured for our salvation, his glorious resurrection and ascension into heaven, and ready to greet him when he comes again, we offer you in thanksgiving this holy and living sacrifice.

Look with favour on your Church's offering and see the victim whose death has reconciled us to yourself. Grant that we who are nourished by his body and blood may be filled with his Holy Spirit, and become one body, one spirit, in Christ. May he make us an everlasting gift to you and enable us to share in the inheritance of your saints, with Mary, the virgin Mother of God, with the apostles, the martyrs and all the saints on whose constant intercession we rely for help.

Lord, may this sacrifice, which has made our peace with you, advance the peace and salvation of all the world. Strengthen in faith and love your pilgrim Church on earth; your servant Pope Benedict, our Archbishop/Bishop and all the bishops, with the clergy and the entire people your Son has gained for you.

Father, hear the prayers of the family you have gathered here before you. In mercy and love unite all your children wherever they may be. Welcome into your kingdom our departed brothers and sisters and all who have left this world in your friendship.

We hope to enjoy forever the vision of your glory, through Christ our Lord, from whom all good things come.

Through him,

with him,

in him,

in the unity of the Holy Spirit,

all glory and honour is yours, Almighty Father,

For ever and ever.

P.   Amen.

Communion Rite

C.   When Jesus walked this earth he taught his followers to address
God as 'Father' and so we pray:

P.   Our Father, who art in heaven,
hallowed be thy name.
Thy kingdom come.
Thy will be done on earth, as it is in heaven.
Give us this day our daily bread,
and forgive us our trespasses,
as we forgive those who trespass against us,
and lead us not into temptation,
but deliver us from evil.

Nuptial Blessing

C.   Let us ask God to bless N. and N., now married in Christ, and
unite them in his love through his presence in the Eucharist.

P.   Amen.

Pause for silent prayer.

C.   God our Father, creator of the universe, you made man and
woman in your own likeness and blessed their union. We
humbly pray to you for N. and N., today united in the sacrament of marriage.

May your blessing come upon them. May they find happiness in their love for each other, be blessed with children and
enrich the life of the Church.

May they praise you in their days of happiness and turn to
you in their times of sorrow.

May they know the joy of your help in their work and the
strength of your presence in their need. May they worship you

with the church and be your witnesses in the world. May old age come to them in the company of their friends and may they reach at last the kingdom of heaven.

We ask this through Christ our Lord.

P.   Amen.

Rite of Peace

C.   Lord Jesus Christ, you said to your apostles: I leave you peace, my peace I give you. Look not on our sins but on the faith of the Church, and grant us the peace and unity of your kingdom where you live for ever and ever.

P.   Amen.

C.   The peace of the Lord be with you always.

P.   And also with you.

C.   Let us offer each other the sign of peace.

P.   Lamb of God, you take away the sins of the world: have mercy on us.

Lamb of God, you take away the sins of the world: have mercy on us.

Lamb of God, you take away the sins of the world: grant us peace.

C.   This is the Lamb of God who takes away the sins of the world. Happy are those who are called to his table.

P   Lord, I am not worthy to receive you, but only say the word and I shall be healed.

Communion Reflection

You are a man and woman of love. You bring to this wedding ceremony all that you are and all that has made you who you are: your families, your friends, your giftedness, your experience of life, your insights and your wisdom. You bring your hopes and your dreams of what shared love might be.

In your love for each other we see the Spirit of Love and Life in human form and we rejoice in the wonderful ways each of you makes that Spirit visible to us. Be always the man and the woman you are because that is what delights and attracts you and brings you together. It is also what we, your family and friends, delight in.

But let there also be space and room for the other to grow as you form a bond this day that you may wish to be unending and unbreakable. May that bonding be joyful and gracious. May your love be overflowing and generous.

In all the years to come may you delightedly be N. and N., wife and husband, strong and constant in love for each other, for your families and for your friends.

Prayer after Communion

C.   Lord, we who have shared the food of your table pray for our friends N. and N. who you have joined together in marriage. Keep them close to you always. May their love for each other proclaim to all the world their faith in you.
We ask this through Christ our Lord.

P.   Amen.

Concluding Rite

C.   The Lord be with you.

P.   And also with you.

C.   May God the Eternal Father keep you steadfast in your love.

P.   Amen.

C.   May you have children to bless you, friends to console you and may you live in peace with all.

P.   Amen.

C.   May you bear witness to the love of God. May the suffering and poor find you generous and welcome you one day into our Father's kingdom.

P.   Amen.

C.   May the peace of Christ ever dwell in your home. May the angels of God protect it and may the holy family of Nazareth be its model and inspiration.

P.   Amen.

C.   May almighty God bless you, the Father and the Son and the Holy Spirit.

P.   Amen.

C.   Let us go from here in peace and in love to continue our celebration.

P.   Thanks be to God.

Signing of the Register

Recessional

A WEDDING CELEBRATION WITHOUT NUPTIAL MASS

Entrance Music and/or Hymn

The priest/minister may initially greet the couple as they arrive together in the sanctuary area of the church. If it has been decided to include the candle ceremony, he invites them to each take a light from the altar candles and light their respective candles, which symbolise their unique identity.

C.   In the name of the Father and of the Son and of the Holy Spirit.

P.   Amen.

C.   The grace of our Lord Jesus Christ and the love of God and the fellowship of the Holy Spirit be with you all.

P.   And also with you.

The whole congregation are now welcomed.

Penitential Rite

C.   As we come together on this joyous occasion to celebrate God's sealing of N. and N.'s love in the sacrament of matrimony, we turn to our all-loving God with trust and confidence.

      Love is your very nature:
      Lord have mercy.

P.   Lord have mercy.

C.   Our deepest call in life is to love:
      Christ have mercy.

P.   Christ have mercy.

C.   For the times we do not live up to this call:
      Lord have mercy.

P.   Lord have mercy.

C.   May almighty God have mercy on us, forgive us our sins and bring us to everlasting life.

P.   Amen.

Gloria

Glory to God in the highest,
and peace to his people on earth.
Lord God, heavenly King,
Almighty God and Father.
We worship you, we give you thanks, we praise you for your glory.
Lord Jesus Christ, only Son of the Father,
Lord God, Lamb of God,
you take away the sins of the world:
Have mercy on us.
You are seated at the right hand of the Father:
Receive our prayer.
For you alone are the Holy One.
You alone are the Lord.

You alone are the Most High,
Jesus Christ,
With the Holy Spirit,
In the glory of God the Father. Amen

Opening Prayer

C.   Let us pray.

The congregation is invited to pray in silence for a moment.

C.   Father, when you created humankind, you willed that man and wife should be one.

Bind N. and N. in the loving union of marriage, and make their love fruitful, so that they may be living witnesses, to your divine love in the world.

We ask this through our Lord Jesus Christ, your Son, who lives and reigns with you and the Holy Spirit, one God, for ever and ever.

P.   Amen.

Liturgy of the Word

First Reading

R.   *A reading from the Book of Ruth (1:16-17)*
Ruth said: 'Do not press me to leave you or to turn back from following you! Where you go, I will go; where you lodge, I will lodge: your people shall be my people and your God my God. Where you die, I will die – there I will be buried. May the Lord do thus and so to me and more as well, if even death parts me from you!'

This is the word of the Lord.

P.   Thanks be to God.

Psalm (Sung)

Psalm 32 (if recited)

Response: The Lord fills the earth with his love

R.   They are happy, whose God is the Lord,
the people he has chosen as his own.
The Lord looks on those who revere him,
on those who hope in his love.   *Response*

Our soul is waiting for the Lord.
The Lord is our help and our shield.
In him do our hearts find joy.
We trust in his holy name.   *Response*

May your love be upon us, O Lord,
as we place all our hope in you.   *Response*

Second Reading

R.   *A reading from the letter of St Paul to the Corinthians (13:1-8)*
If I speak in the tongues of mortals and angels, but do not have love, I am a noisy gong or a clanging cymbal. And if I have prophetic powers and understand all mysteries and all knowledge and if I have all faith so as to remove mountains, but do not have love, I am nothing. If I give away all my possessions and if I hand over my body so that I may boast, but do not have love, I gain nothing.

    Love is patient, love is kind, love is not envious or boastful or arrogant or rude. It does not insist on its own way, it is not irritable or resentful; it does not rejoice in wrongdoing, but rejoices in the truth. It bears all things, believes all things, hopes all things, endures all things.

    Love never ends. But as for prophecies, they will come to an end; as for tongues, they will cease; as for knowledge, it will come to an end. For we know only in part; but when the complete comes, the partial will come to an end.

This is the word of the Lord.

P.   Thanks be to God.

Gospel Acclamation

Alleluia (sung)

Gospel

C.   The Lord be with you.
P.   And also with you.
C.   A reading from the Holy Gospel according to Mark (10:6-9).
P.   Glory to you O Lord.
C.   Jesus said to them: 'From the beginning of creation God made them male and female. For this reason a man shall leave his father and mother and be joined to his wife and the two shall become one flesh. So they are no longer two but one flesh. Therefore, what God has joined together, let no one separate.'

This is the Gospel of the Lord.

P.   Praise to you Lord Jesus Christ.

Homily

Rite of Marriage

C.   Dear Children of God,
You have come to this church so that the Lord may seal your love in the presence of the priest/minister and this community. Christ blesses this love. He has already consecrated you

in baptism; now by a special sacrament, he strengthens you to fulfil the duties of your married life.

N. and N., you are about to celebrate this sacrament.

Have you come here of your own free will and choice and without compulsion to marry each other?

Both   We have.

C.   Will you love and honour each other in marriage all the days of your life?

Both   We will.

C.   Are you willing to accept with love the children God may send you and bring them up in accordance with the law of Christ and his Church?

Both   We are.

Declaration of Consent

C.   I invite you then to declare before God and his Church your consent to become husband and wife.

Bride and groom join hands:

G.   I, N., take you N. as my wife,
       In friendship and in love,
       To have and to hold from this day forward.
       I promise to be true to you
       In good times and in bad,
       In sickness and in health.
       I will love and cherish you all the days of my life.

B.   I, N., take you N. as my husband,
       In friendship and in love,
       To have and to hold from this day forward.
       I promise to be true to you
       In good times and in bad,
       In sickness and in health.
       I will love and cherish you all the days of my life.

When the bride and groom have given their consent, the priest/minister says:

C.   What God joins together, no one should separate. May the Lord confirm the consent that you have given and enrich you with his blessing.
or
The Lord has joined you together.
May he fulfil his blessing in you;
May he keep you in his love.

Blessing of Rings

C.   Almighty God, bless these rings, symbols of faithfulness and unbroken love. May N. and N. always be true to each other. May they be one in heart and mind. May they be united in love forever.
Through Christ our Lord.

P.   Amen.

Exchange of Rings

The groom places a ring on the bride's finger saying:

G.   N., wear this ring as a sign of our friendship and faithful love.
In the name of the Father and of the Son and of the Holy Spirit.
Amen.

The bride then places a ring on the groom's finger saying:

B.   N., wear this ring as a sign of our friendship and faithful love.
In the name of the Father and of the Son and of the Holy Spirit.
Amen.

The bride and groom may exchange small symbolic gifts, each saying:

G.   N., I give you this gift, a token of all I possess.

B.   N., I give you this gift, a token of all I possess.

Together N. and N. light a single candle from the two which they lit at the beginning of the liturgy, as a symbol of their union as husband and wife.

Prayer of the Newly Married Couple (Optional)

We thank you, Lord,

and we praise you

for bringing us

to this happy day.

You have given us each other.

Now, together, we give ourselves to you.

We ask you, Lord:

make us one in our love.

Keep us one in your peace.

Protect our marriage.

Bless our home.

Make us gentle

Keep us faithful.

And when life is over

unite us again

where parting is no more

in the kingdom of your love.

There we will praise you

in the happiness and peace

of our eternal home.

Amen.

General Intercessions/Prayers of the Faithful

C.   God has given us the promise of fidelity and love in the Word of Scripture. N. and N. have given their promise of life-long faithful love in the Sacrament of Marriage. This hour of promise is also a time of prayer.

We turn to God with confidence.

R.   For N. and N. as they set out on a new journey today as husband and wife, that the beauty of their love for each other may be a reflection of the ebb and flow of the divine–human relationship.
Lord hear us.

P.   Lord graciously hear us.

R.   As N. and N. bring to this wedding ceremony all that has made them who they are, we pray for their parents, family members and friends and all who have helped them reach this pinnacle of love.
Lord hear us.

P.   Lord graciously hear us.

R.   That all Church leaders proclaim that the very nature of God is one of self-giving love, a love that we are all called to imitate.
Lord hear us.

P.   Lord graciously hear us.

R.   That all peoples of the world may experience a new reality where family life is cherished and children grow up in security, love and peace.
Lord hear us.

P.   Lord graciously hear us.

R.   For all who need our prayers and are in our thoughts today, that they may experience the caring presence of God in their lives.
Lord hear us.

P.   Lord graciously hear us.

R. For all who have died and especially for those whom we have known and loved, that God will one day unite us again in the joys of our eternal home.
Lord hear us.

P. Lord graciously hear us.

C. O ever-loving and caring God, as we celebrate this sacramental moment in the lives of N. and N., we pray that their love may continue to deepen as they journey though life together.

P. Amen.

C. When Jesus walked this earth he taught his followers to address God as 'Father', and so we pray with loving trust and confidence:

P. Our Father, who art in heaven,
hallowed be thy name.
Thy kingdom come.
Thy will be done on earth, as it is in heaven.
Give us this day our daily bread,
and forgive us our trespasses,
as we forgive those who trespass against us,
and lead us not into temptation,
but deliver us from evil.

Hymn/Reflective Music

Nuptial Blessing

C. Let us ask God to bless N. and N., now married in Christ, and unite them in love.

P. Amen.

Pause for silent prayer.

C. Father, you created the universe and made man and woman in your own likeness. You gave woman as companion to man, so that they should no longer be two, but one flesh, teaching us that those you have so united may never be separated.

Father, you have sanctified marriage in a mystery so holy that it is a sign of the union of Christ and the Church. Look with love upon N., as she asks your blessing. May she live in peace with you and follow the example of those women whose lives are praised in the scriptures.

May N. place his trust in her and see her as his companion. May he always honour her and love her as Christ loves the Church.

Father, keep this husband and wife strong in faith and true to your commandments. May they be faithful to each other, examples of Christian living and witnesses of Christ. Bless them with children and help them to be good parents. And after a long and happy life together may they enjoy the company of your saints in heaven.

We ask this through Christ our Lord.

P.   Amen.

Reflection

One night a man had a dream. He dreamed he was walking along the beach with the Lord. Across the sky flashed scenes from his life. For each scene, he noticed two sets of footprints in the sand: one belonging to him and the other to the Lord.

When the last scene of his life flashed before him, he looked back at the footprints in the sand. He noticed that many times along the path of his life there was only one set of footprints. He also noticed that it happened at the very lowest and saddest times in his life. This really bothered him and he questioned the Lord about it.

'Lord, you said that once I decided to follow you, you'd walk with me all the way. But I have noticed that during the most troublesome times in my life there is only one set of footprints. I don't understand why, when I needed you most, you would leave me.'

The Lord replied, 'My precious, precious child, I love you and I would never leave you. During your times of trial and suffering, when you see only one set of footprints, it was then I carried you'.

Concluding Rite

C.   The Lord be with you.

P.   And also with you.

Before blessing the general congregation the priest/minister gives the bride and groom a special blessing.

C.   May God, the Almighty Father, grant you his joy: may he bless you in your children.

P.   Amen.

C.   May Jesus Christ, the Son of God, in his mercy help you in good times and in bad.

P.   Amen.

C.   May the Holy Spirit of God always fill you with his love.

P.   Amen.

Blessing and Dismissal

C.   May almighty God bless you all, the Father and the Son and the Holy Spirit.

P.   Amen.

C.   Let us all go in the peace of Christ.

P.   Thanks be to God.

SECTION II

PERSONALISE YOUR WEDDING CEREMONY

This section of the book offers various options from which to choose in order to personalise your own wedding ceremony.

INTRODUCTORY RITE

Most wedding liturgies begin with music or a hymn. On the rare occasion where there is no music or song it is customary to commence with an entrance antiphon, such as one of the following. This helps to focus people's attention on what is about to happen.

Ps 19:3, 5

May the Lord send you help from his holy place and from Zion may he watch over you. May he grant you your heart's desire and lend aid to all your plans.

Ps 89:14, 17

Fill us with your love, O Lord, and we will sing for joy all our days. May the goodness of the Lord be upon us, and give success to the work of our hands.

Ps 114:2, 9

Lord, I will bless you day after day, and praise your name forever; for you are kind to all and compassionate to all your creatures.

C.   In the name of the Father and of the Son and of the Holy Spirit.
P.   Amen.

The priest/minister greets everyone. He may use one of the following sacred greetings:

C.   The grace of our Lord Jesus Christ and the love of God and the fellowship of the Holy Spirit be with you all.
P.   And also with you.

C.   The grace and peace of God our Father and the Lord Jesus Christ be with you.
P.   And also with you.

C.   The Lord be with you.

P.   And also be with you.

PENITENTIAL RITE

The Penitential Rite is introduced by a, b or c, or perhaps more informally.

a.   My brothers and sisters, to prepare ourselves to celebrate the sacred mysteries, let us call to mind our sins.

b.   As we prepare to celebrate the mystery of Christ's love, let us acknowledge our failures and ask the Lord for pardon and strength.

c.   Coming together as God's family, with confidence let us ask the Father's forgiveness, for he is full of gentleness and compassion.

After a brief silence one of the following is used:

C.   Lord Jesus, you came to reconcile us to one another and to the Father:
     Lord have mercy.

P.   Lord have mercy.

C.   Lord Jesus, you heal the wounds of sin and division:
     Christ have mercy.

P.   Christ have mercy.

C.   Lord Jesus, you intercede for us with your Father:
     Lord have mercy.

P.   Lord have mercy.

The priest says the absolution:

C.   May almighty God have mercy on us, forgive us our sins and bring us to everlasting life.

P.   Amen.

C.   Lord Jesus, you have shown us the way to the Father:
Lord have mercy.

P.   Lord have mercy.

C.   Lord Jesus you have given us the consolation of the truth:
Christ have mercy.

P.   Christ have mercy.

C.   Lord Jesus, you are the Good Shepherd, leading us into everlasting life:
Lord have mercy.

P.   Lord have mercy.

The priest says the absolution:

C.   May almighty God have mercy on us, forgive us our sins and bring us to everlasting life.

P.   Amen.

C.   Lord Jesus, you raise us to new life:
Lord, have mercy.

P.   Lord, have mercy.

C.   Lord Jesus, you forgive us our sins:
Christ, have mercy.

P.   Christ, have mercy.

C.   Lord Jesus, you nourish us with the Eucharist:
Lord, have mercy.

P.   Lord, have mercy.

The priest says the absolution:

C.   May almighty God have mercy on us, forgive us our sins and bring us to everlasting life.

P.   Amen.

C.   Lord Jesus, you healed the sick:
       Lord, have mercy.

P.   Lord, have mercy.

C.   Lord Jesus, you forgave sinners:
       Christ, have mercy.

P.   Christ, have mercy.

C.   Lord Jesus, you give us yourself in the Eucharist to heal us and bring us strength:
       Lord, have mercy.

P.   Lord, have mercy.

The priest says the absolution:

C.   May almighty God have mercy on us, forgive us our sins and bring us to everlasting life.

P.   Amen.

C.   Lord Jesus, you came to gather the nations into the peace of God's kingdom:
       Lord, have mercy.

P.   Lord, have mercy.

C.   You come in word and sacrament to strengthen us in holiness:
       Christ, have mercy.

P.   Christ, have mercy.

C.   You will come in glory with salvation for your people:
       Lord, have mercy.

P.   Lord have mercy.

The priest says the absolution:

C.   May almighty God have mercy on us, forgive us our sins and bring us to everlasting life.

P.   Amen.

C.   Lord Jesus, you are mighty God and Prince of peace:
Lord, have mercy.

P.   Lord, have mercy.

C.   Lord Jesus, you are Son of God and Son of Mary:
Christ, have mercy.

P.   Christ, have mercy.

C.   Lord Jesus, you are Word made flesh and splendour of the Father:
Lord, have mercy.

P.   Lord, have mercy.

The priest says the absolution:

C.   May almighty God have mercy on us, forgive us our sins and bring us to everlasting life.

P.   Amen.

C.   You were sent to heal the contrite:
Lord, have mercy.

P.   Lord, have mercy.

C.   You came to call sinners:
Christ, have mercy.

P.   Christ, have mercy.

C.   You plead for us at the right hand of the Father:
Lord, have mercy.

P.   Lord, have mercy.

The priest says the absolution:

C.   May almighty God have mercy on us, forgive us our sins and bring us to everlasting life.

P.   Amen.

C.   You raise the dead to life in the Spirit:
Lord, have mercy.

P.   Lord, have mercy.
C.   You bring pardon and peace to the sinner:
     Christ, have mercy.
P.   Christ, have mercy.
C.   You bring light to those in darkness:
     Lord, have mercy.
P.   Lord, have mercy.

The priest says the absolution:

C.   May almighty God have mercy on us, forgive us our sins and
     bring us to everlasting life.
P.   Amen.

GLORIA

Glory to God in the highest,
and peace to his people on earth.
Lord God, heavenly King,
Almighty God and Father.
We worship you, we give you thanks, we praise you for your glory.
Lord Jesus Christ, only Son of the Father,
Lord God, Lamb of God,
you take away the sins of the world:
Have mercy on us.
You are seated at the right hand of the Father:
Receive our prayer.
For you alone are the Holy One.
You alone are the Lord.
You alone are the Most High,
Jesus Christ,
With the Holy Spirit,
In the glory of God the Father. Amen.

OPENING PRAYER

The priest/minister invites the wedding party and guests to pray silently for a moment. This is followed by a prayer. You may choose one of the four that follow:

Prayer 1

Father, you have made the bond of marriage a holy mystery, a symbol of Christ's love for his Church. Hear our prayers for N. and N. With faith in you and in each other they pledge their love today. May their lives always bear witness to the reality of that love. We ask this through our Lord Jesus Christ, your Son, who lives and reigns with you and the Holy Spirit, one God, for ever and ever. Amen.

Prayer 2

Father, when you created mankind you willed that man and wife should be one. Bind N. and N. in the loving union of marriage and make their love fruitful so that they may be living witnesses to your divine love in the world. We ask this through our Lord Jesus Christ, your Son, who lives and reigns with you and the Holy Spirit, one God, for ever and ever. Amen.

Prayer 3

Almighty God, hear our prayers for N. and N. who have come here today to be united in the sacrament of marriage. Increase their faith in you and in each other and through them bless your Church (with Christian children). We ask this through our Lord Jesus Christ, your Son, who lives and reigns with you and the Holy Spirit, one God, for ever and ever. Amen.

Prayer 4

Father, hear our prayers for N. and N. who today are united in marriage before your altar. Give them your blessing and strengthen their love for each other. We ask this through our Lord Jesus Christ, your

Son, who lives and reigns with you and the Holy Spirit, one God, for ever and ever. Amen.

LITURGY OF THE WORD

The Liturgy of the Word comprises a set of readings from the Bible. The first reading is usually taken from the Old Testament; this is followed by a psalm (preferably sung). The second scripture passage is taken from the New Testament. After this reading, all stand to greet the Gospel with the Alleluia verse, which immediately precedes a passage from one of the four gospels – Matthew, Mark, Luke or John.

Old Testament Readings

You may wonder what relevance the Old Testament has for our time and more particularly for your love relationship. Yet, much of the wisdom contained in passages from the Old Testament is as relevant today as it was more than two thousand years ago. Just think of the reading about friendship in the sample wedding ceremony given at the beginning of this book. Christians believe that here God speaks to us, offering wisdom for living life in a meaningful, fulfilled and happy manner.

A Reading from the Book of Sirach (6:14-17)
Faithful friends are a sturdy shelter; whoever finds one has found a treasure. Faithful friends are beyond price: no amount can balance their worth. Faithful friends are life-saving medicine and those who fear the Lord will find them. Those who fear the Lord direct their friendship aright, for as they are, so are their neighbours also.

A Reading from the Book of Ruth (1:16-18)
Ruth said: 'Do not press me to leave you or to turn back from following you! Where you go, I will go; where you lodge, I will lodge: your people shall be my people and your God my God. Where you die, I will die –

there I will be buried. May the Lord do thus and so to me and more as well, if even death parts me from you!'

When Naomi saw that she was determined to go with her, she said no more to her.

A Reading from the Book of Genesis (1:26-28, 31)

Then God said: 'Let us make humankind in our image, according to our likeness and let them have dominion over the fish of the sea, and over all the wild animals of the earth and over every creeping thing that creeps upon the earth.'

So God created humankind in his image, in the image of God he created them, male and female he created them.

God blessed them and God said to them: 'Be fruitful and multiply and fill the earth and subdue it; and have dominion over the fish of the sea and over the birds of the air and over every living thing that moves upon the earth.'

God saw everything that he had made and indeed it was very good.

A Reading from the Prophet Isaiah (43:1-2)

But now thus says the Lord, he who created you, he who formed you, 'Do not fear for I have redeemed you; I have called you by name, you are mine. When you pass through the waters, I will be with you; and through the rivers, they shall not overwhelm you; when you walk through fire you shall not be burned, and the flame shall not consume you. For I am the Lord your God, the Holy One of Israel, your Saviour. You are precious in my sight and honoured and I love you.'

A Reading from the Prophet Isaiah (61:10-11)

I will greatly rejoice in the Lord, my whole being shall exult in my God; for he has clothed me with the garments of salvation, he has covered me with the robe of righteousness, as a bridegroom decks himself with a garland, and as a bride adorns herself with her jewels. For as the earth brings forth its shoots and as a garden causes what is sown in it to spring up, so the Lord God will cause righteousness and praise to spring up before all the nations.

A Reading from the Book of Genesis (2:18-25)

Then the Lord God said: 'It is not good that man should be alone; I will make him a helper as his partner.' So out of the ground the Lord God formed every animal of the field and every bird of the air and brought them to the man to see what he would call them; and whatever the man called each living creature, that was its name. The man gave names to all cattle and to the birds of the air and to every animal of the field; but for the man there was not found a helper as his partner. So the Lord God caused a deep sleep to fall upon the man and he slept; then he took one of his ribs and closed up its place with flesh. And the rib that the Lord God had taken from the man he made into a woman and brought her to the man.

Then the man said, 'This at last is bone of my bones and flesh of my flesh; this one shall be called woman for out of man this one was taken'. Therefore a man leaves his father and his mother and clings to his wife and they become one flesh. And the man and his wife were both naked and were not ashamed.

A Reading from the Song of Solomon (2:10-14)

My beloved speaks and says to me: 'Arise my love, my fair one, and come away, for now the winter is past, the rain is over and gone. The flowers appear on the earth; the time of singing has come and the voice of the turtle-dove is heard in our land. The fig tree puts forth its figs and the vines are in blossom; they give forth fragrance. Arise my love, my fair one, and come away. Let me see your face, let me hear your voice, for your voice is sweet and your face is lovely.'

A Reading from the Song of Solomon (8:6-7)

Set me as a seal upon your heart, as a seal upon your arm; for love is strong as death, passion fierce as the grave. Its flashes are flashes of fire, a raging flame. Many waters cannot quench love, neither can floods drown it. If one offered for love all the wealth of one's house, it would be utterly scorned.

A Reading from the Prophet Isaiah (54:5, 6a,7-10)

Your maker is your husband. The Lord of hosts is his name. The Holy One of Israel is your Redeemer, the God of the whole earth he is called. For the Lord has called you. For a brief moment I abandoned you, but with great compassion I will gather you. With everlasting love I will have compassion on you, says the Lord, your Redeemer. This is like the days of Noah to me: just as I swore that the waters of Noah would never again go over the earth, so have I sworn that I will not be angry with you and will not rebuke you. For the mountains may depart and the hills be removed, but my steadfast love shall not depart from you and my covenant of peace shall not be removed, says the Lord, who has compassion on you.

A Reading from the Book of Tobit (8:4-8)

When the parents had gone out and shut the door of the room, Tobias got out of bed and said to Sarah, 'Sister, get up and let us pray and implore our Lord that he grant us mercy and safety'. So she got up and they began to pray and implore that they might be kept safe. Tobias began by saying, 'Blessed are you, O God of our ancestors, and blessed is your name in all generations for ever. Let the heavens and the whole creation bless you for ever. You made Adam, and for him you made his wife Eve as a helper and support. From the two of them the human race has sprung. You said, 'It is not good that the man should be alone; let us make a helper for him like himself'. I now am taking this kinswoman of mine, not because of lust, but with sincerity. Grant that she and I may find mercy and that we may grow old together.' And they both said, 'Amen, Amen'. Then they went to sleep for the night.

Psalms

Psalm 32

The response is: The Lord fills the earth with his love!

They are happy, whose God is the Lord,
the people he has chosen as his own.
The Lord looks on those who revere him
on those who hope in his love.   *Response*

Our soul is waiting for the Lord.
The Lord is our help and our shield.
In him do our hearts find joy.
We trust in his holy name.   *Response*

May your love be upon us, O Lord,
as we place all our hope in you.   *Response*

Psalm 33

*The response is either: I will bless the Lord at all times OR Taste and see that the
Lord is good*

I will bless the Lord at all times,
his praise always on my lips.
In the Lord my soul shall make its boast.
The humble shall hear and be glad.   *Response*

Glorify the Lord with me.
Together let us praise his name.
I sought the Lord and he answered me;
from all my terrors he set me free.   *Response*

Look towards him and be radiant;
let your faces not be abashed.
This poor man called; the Lord heard him
and rescued him from all his distress.   *Response*

The angel of the Lord is encamped
around those who revere him, to rescue them.
Taste and see that the Lord is good.
He is happy who seeks refuge in him.   *Response*

Psalm 102

The response is: The Lord is compassion and love

My soul, give thanks to the Lord,
all my being, bless his holy name.
My soul, give thanks to the Lord
and never forget all his blessings.   *Response*

The Lord is compassion and love,
slow to anger and rich in mercy.
As a father has compassion on his sons,
the Lord has pity on those who fear him.   *Response*

The love of the Lord is everlasting
upon those who hold him in fear;
His justice reaches out to their children's children
when they keep his covenant in truth.   *Response*

Psalm 111

The response is either: Happy the man who takes delight in the Lord's commands OR Alleluia

Happy the man who fears the Lord,
who takes delight in his commands;
his sons will be powerful on earth;
the children of the upright are blessed.   *Response*

Riches and wealth are in his house;
his justice stands firm for ever.
He is a light in the darkness for the upright;
he is generous, merciful and just.   *Response*

The good man takes pity and lends,
he conducts his affairs with honour.
The just man will never waver:
he will be remembered for ever.   *Response*

He has no fears of evil news;
with a firm heart he trusts in the Lord.
With a steadfast heart he will not fear;
he will see the downfall of his foes.   *Response*

Open-handed, he gives to the poor;
his justice stands firm for ever.
His head will be raised in glory.   *Response*

Psalm 127

The response is either: Blessed are those who fear the Lord OR Indeed thus shall be blessed the one who fears the Lord

O blessed are those who fear the Lord
and walk in his ways!
By the labour of your hands you shall eat.
You will be happy and prosper.   *Response*

Your wife shall be like a fruitful vine
In the heart of your house,
your children like shoots of the olive
around your table.   *Response*

Indeed thus shall be blessed
the man who fears the Lord.
May the Lord bless you from Zion
all the days of your life!   *Response*

Psalm 144

The response is: How good is the Lord to all!

The Lord is kind and full of compassion,
slow to anger, abounding in love.
How good is the Lord to all,
compassionate to all his creatures.   *Response*

All your creatures shall thank you, O Lord,
and your friends shall repeat their blessing.
The eyes of all creatures look to you
and you give them their food in due time.   *Response*

The Lord is just in all his ways,
and loving in all his deeds.
He is close to all who call him,
who call on him from their hearts.   *Response*

Psalm 148

The response is either: Praise the name of the Lord OR Alleluia

Praise the Lord from the heavens,
praise him in the heights.

Praise him, all his angels,
praise him, all his host!   *Response*

Praise him, sun and moon;
praise him, shining stars.
Praise him, highest heavens,
and the waters above the heavens.   *Response*

All mountains and hills
all fruit trees and cedars,
beasts, wild and tame,
reptiles and birds on the wing.   *Response*

All earth's kings and peoples,
earth's princes and rulers;
young men and maidens,
old men together with children.   *Response*

Let them praise the name of the Lord,
for he alone is exalted.
The splendour of his name
reaches beyond heaven and earth.   *Response*

Psalm 102

The response is: The Lord is compassion and love

The Lord is compassion and love,
slow to anger and rich in mercy.
He does not treat us according to our sins
nor repay us according to our faults.   *Response*

For as the heavens are high above the earth
so strong is his love for those who fear him.

As far as the east is from the west
so far does he remove our sins.   *Response*

As a father has compassion on his children
the Lord has pity on those who fear him;
for he knows of what we are made,
he remembers that we are dust.   *Response*

The love of the Lord is everlasting
upon those who fear him;
his justice reaches out to children's children
when they keep his covenant in truth.   *Response*

Psalm 137

The response is: Your love, O Lord, is eternal

I thank you, Lord, with all my heart.
You have heard the words of my mouth.
Before the angels I will bless you.
I will adore before your holy temple.   *Response*

I thank you for your faithfulness and love,
which excel all we ever knew of you.
On the day I called, you answered;
you increased the strength of my soul.   *Response*

You stretch out your hand and save me,
your hand will do all things for me.
Your love, O Lord, is eternal,
discard not the work of your hands.   *Response*

Psalm 120

The response is: My help shall come from the Lord who made heaven and earth

I lift up my eyes to the mountains:
From where shall come my help?
My help shall come from the Lord,
who made heaven and earth.   *Response*

May he never allow you to stumble.
Let him sleep not, your guard.
No, he sleeps not nor slumbers,
Israel's guard.   *Response*

The Lord is your guard and your shade;
at your right side he stands.
By day the sun shall not smite you,
nor the moon in the night.   *Response*

The Lord will guard you from evil,
he will guard your soul.
The Lord will guard your going and coming,
both now and for ever.   *Response*

Psalm 99

The response is: The Lord is faithful from age to age

Cry out with joy to the Lord all the earth.
Serve the Lord with gladness,
come before him, singing for joy.   *Response*

Know that he, the Lord, is God.
He made us, we belong to him,
we are his people, the sheep of his flock.   *Response*

Go within his gates, giving thanks.
Enter his courts with songs of praise.
Give thanks to him and bless his name.   *Response*

Indeed, how good is the Lord,
eternal his merciful love.
He is faithful from age to age.   *Response*

Psalm 26

The response is: The Lord is my light and my help

The Lord is my light and my help;
whom shall I fear?
The Lord is the stronghold of my life;
before whom shall I shrink?   *Response*

There is one thing I ask of the Lord,
for this I long:
to live in the house of the Lord
all the days of my life.   *Response*

Do not abandon or forsake me,
O God my help.
Though father and mother forsake me,
the Lord will receive me.   *Response*

I am sure I shall see the Lord's goodness
in the land of the living.
Hope in him, hold firm and take heart.
Hope in the Lord.   *Response*

Psalm 32

The response is: May your love be upon us, O Lord, as we place all our hope in you

They are happy, whose God is the Lord,
the people he has chosen as his own.
From the heavens the Lord looks forth,
he sees all the children of men.   *Response*

From the place where he dwells he gazes
on all the dwellers on the earth,
he who shapes the hearts of them all
and considers all their deeds.   *Response*

The Lord looks on those who revere him,
on those who hope in his love
to rescue their souls from death,
to keep them alive in famine.   *Response*

Our soul is waiting for the Lord.
The Lord is our help and our shield.
In him do our hearts find joy.
We trust in his holy name.   *Response*

Psalm 61

The response is: In God alone is my soul at rest

In God alone is my soul at rest;
my help comes from him.
He alone is my rock, my stronghold,
my fortress: I stand firm.   *Response*

Take refuge in God all you people;
trust him at all times.

Pour out your heart before him,
for God is our refuge.   *Response*

Do not put your trust in oppression
nor vain hopes of plunder.
Do not set your heart on riches,
even when they increase.   *Response*

For God has said only one thing:
only two do I know:
that to God alone belongs power,
and to you, Lord, love.   *Response*

Psalm 91

The response is: It is good to give thanks to the Lord

It is good to give thanks to the Lord,
to make music to your name, O Most High,
to proclaim your love in the morning
and your truth in the watches of the night.   *Response*

Your deeds, O Lord, have made me glad;
for the work of your hands I shout with joy.
O Lord, how great are your works,
how deep are your designs.   *Response*

The just will flourish like the palm-tree
and grow like a Lebanon cedar.
Planted in the House of the Lord
they will flourish in the courts of our God.   *Response*

Still bearing fruit when they are old,
still full of sap, still green,

to proclaim that the Lord is just;
in him, my rock, there is no wrong.   *Response*

New Testament Readings

A Reading from the First Letter of St Paul to the Corinthians (12:31-13:8)

And I will show you a still more excellent way. If I speak in the tongues of mortals and of angels, but do not have love, I am a noisy gong or a clanging cymbal. And if I have prophetic powers and understand all mysteries and all knowledge and if I have all faith so as to remove mountains, but do not have love, I am nothing. If I give away all my possessions and if I hand over my body so that I may boast, but do not have love, I gain nothing.

Love is patient; love is kind; love is not envious or boastful or arrogant or rude. It does not insist on its own way; it is not irritable or resentful; it does not rejoice in wrongdoing but rejoices in the truth. It bears all things, believes all things, hopes all things, endures all things. Love never ends.

This is the word of the Lord.

P.   Thanks be to God.

A Reading from the Letter of St Paul to the Colossians (3:12-17)

As God's chosen ones, holy and beloved, clothe yourselves with compassion, kindness, humility, meekness and patience. Bear with one another and if anyone has a complaint against another, forgive each other; just as the Lord has forgiven you, so you also must forgive. Above all, clothe yourselves with love which binds everything together in perfect harmony. And let the peace of Christ rule in your hearts, to which indeed you were called in the one body. And be thankful. Let the word of Christ dwell in you richly; teach and admonish one another in all wisdom; and with gratitude in your hearts sing psalms, hymns and spiritual songs to

God. And whatever you do, in word or deed, do everything in the name of the Lord Jesus, giving thanks to God the Father through him.

This is the word of the Lord.

P.   Thanks be to God.

A Reading from the First Letter of St John (3:18-24)

Little children, let us love, not in word or speech, but in truth and action. And by this we will know that we are from the truth and will reassure our hearts before him whenever our hearts condemn us; for God is greater than our hearts, and he knows everything. Beloved, if our hearts do not condemn us, we have boldness before God; and we receive from him whatever we ask because we obey his commandments and do what pleases him. And this is his commandment: that we should believe in the name of his Son Jesus Christ and love one another, just as he has commanded us. All who obey his commandments abide in him, and he abides in them. And by this we know that he abides in us by the Spirit that he has given us.

This is the word of the Lord.

P.   Thanks be to God.

A Reading from the First Letter of St John (4:7-12)

Beloved, let us love one another, because love is from God; everyone who loves is born of God and knows God. Whoever does not love does not know God, for God is love. God's love was revealed among us in this way: God sent his only Son into the world so that we might live through him. In this is love, not that we loved God but that he loved us and sent his Son to be the atoning sacrifice for our sins. Beloved, since God loved us so much, we also ought to love one another. No one has ever seen God; if we love one another, God lives in us and his love is perfected in us.

This is the word of the Lord.

P.   Thanks be to God.

A Reading from the Letter of St Paul to the Romans (12:9-12)

Let love be genuine, hate what is evil, hold fast to what is good; love one another with mutual affection; outdo one another in showing honour. Do not lag in zeal; be ardent in spirit, serve the Lord. Rejoice in hope, be patient in suffering, persevere in prayer. Contribute to the needs of God's people, extend hospitality to strangers.

This is the word of the Lord.

P.   Thanks be to God.

A Reading from the Letter of St Paul to the Ephesians (4:1-6)

I therefore beg you to lead a life worthy of the calling to which you have been called with all humility and gentleness, with patience, bearing with one another in love, making every effort to maintain the unity of the Spirit in the bond of peace. There is one body and one Spirit, just as you were called to the one hope of your calling, one Lord, one faith, one baptism, one God and Father of all, who is above all and through all and in all.

This is the word of the Lord.

P.   Thanks be to God.

A Reading from the letter of St Paul to the Romans (15:1-3a, 5-7, 13)

We who are strong ought to put up with the failings of the weak and not to please ourselves. Each of us must please our neighbour for the good purpose of building up the neighbour. For Christ did not please himself. May the God of steadfastness and encouragement grant you to live in harmony with one another; in accordance with Christ Jesus, so that together you may with one voice glorify the God and Father of our Lord Jesus Christ. Welcome one another, therefore, just as Christ has welcomed you, for the glory of God. May the God of hope fill you with all joy and peace in believing so that you may abound in hope by the power of the Holy Spirit.

This is the word of the Lord.

P.   Thanks be to God.

A Reading from the Letter of St Paul to the Philippians (4:4-9)

Rejoice in the Lord always; again I will say, Rejoice. Let your gentleness be known to everyone. The Lord is near. Do not worry about anything but in everything by prayer and supplication with thanksgiving let your requests be made known to God. And the peace of God, which surpasses all understanding, will guard your hearts and your minds in Christ Jesus. Finally, beloved, whatever is true, whatever is honourable, whatever is just, whatever is pure, whatever is pleasing, whatever is commendable, if there is any excellence and if there is anything worthy of praise, think about these things. Keep on doing the things that you have learned and received and heard and seen in me, and the God of peace will be with you.

This is the word of the Lord.

P.   Thanks be to God.

A Reading from the Letter to the Hebrews (13:1-2, 4a-6a)

Let mutual love continue. Do not neglect to show hospitality to strangers, for by doing that, some have entertained angels without knowing it. Let marriage be held in honour by all, and let the marriages be kept undefiled. Keep your lives free from the love of money and be content with what you have; for he has said, 'I will never leave you or forsake you'. So we can say with confidence: the Lord is my helper; I will not be afraid.

This is the word of the Lord.

P.   Thanks be to God.

Gospel Acclamations

If possible, the Gospel Acclamation should always be sung; indeed, it may be omitted if not sung. You may choose from one of the following:

Alleluia Alleluia
As long as we love one another
God will live in us
And his love will be complete in us.
Alleluia.   *(1 John 4:12)*

Alleluia Alleluia
Any one who lives in love
Lives in God
And God lives in them.
Alleluia.   *(1 John 4:16)*

Alleluia Alleluia
God is love
Let us love one another
As God has loved us.
Alleluia.   *(1 John 4:8, 11)*

Alleluia Alleluia
Everyone who loves
Is begotten by God

And knows God.
Alleluia.   *(1 John 4:7)*

'Alleluia' is a phrase in Hebrew, which means 'Praise God!' During the penitential season of Lent we omit the alleluia and verse which may be replaced by a verse such as one of the following:

Praise to you, O Christ, king of eternal glory!
Praise and honour to you Lord Jesus!
Glory and praise to you O Christ!
Glory to you, O Christ; you are the word of God!

Gospel Readings

A Reading from the holy Gospel according to John (15:9-12)
Jesus said to his disciples: 'As the Father has loved me, so have I loved you; abide in my love. If you keep my commandments you will abide in my love, just as I have kept my Father's commandments and abide in his love. I have said these things to you so that my joy may be in you and that your joy may be complete. This is my commandment: that you love one another as I have loved you.'

A Reading from the holy Gospel according to John (15:12-16)
Jesus said to his disciples: 'This is my commandment: that you love one another as I have loved you. No one has greater love than this, to lay down one's life for one's friends. You are my friends if you do what I command you. I do not call you servants any longer, because the servant does not know what the master is doing, but I have called you friends because I have made known to you everything that I have heard from my Father. You did not choose me but I chose you. And I appointed you to go and bear fruit, fruit that will last, so that the Father will give you whatever you ask him in my name. I am giving you these commands so that you may love one another.'

A Reading from the holy Gospel according to Mark (10:6-9)

Jesus said to them: 'From the beginning of creation, God made them male and female. For this reason a man shall leave his father and mother and be joined to his wife and the two shall become one flesh. So they are no longer two but one flesh. Therefore, what God has joined together, let no one separate.'

A Reading from the holy Gospel according to Matthew (22:34-40)

When the Pharisees heard that he had silenced the Sadducees, they gathered together and one of them, a lawyer, asked him a question to test him. 'Teacher, which commandment in the law is the greatest?' He said to him, 'You shall love the Lord your God with all your heart, and with all your soul, and with all your mind. This is the greatest and first commandment. And a second is like it: you shall love your neighbour as yourself. On these two commandments hang all the law and the prophets'.

A Reading from the holy Gospel according to John (2:1-11)

On the third day there was a wedding in Cana of Galilee and the mother of Jesus was there. Jesus and his disciples had also been invited to the wedding. When the wine gave out, the mother of Jesus said to him, 'They have no wine'. Jesus said to her, 'Woman, what concern is that to you and to me? My hour has not yet come'. His mother said to the servants, 'Do whatever he tells you'. Now standing there were six stone water-jars for the Jewish rites of purification, each holding twenty to thirty gallons. Jesus said to them, 'Fill the jars with water,' and they filled them up to the brim. He said to them, 'Now draw some out and take it to the chief steward'. So they took it. When the steward tasted the water that had become wine, and did not know where it came from (though the servants who had drawn the water knew), the steward called the bridegroom and said to him, 'Everyone serves the good wine first, and then the inferior wine after the guests have become drunk. But you have kept the good wine until now'. Jesus did this, the first of his signs, in Cana of Galilee, and revealed his glory and his disciples believed in him.

A Reading from the holy Gospel according to John (17:20-23)

Jesus raised his eyes to heaven and said: 'Father I ask not only on behalf of these, but also on behalf of those who will believe in me through their word, that they may all be one. As you, Father, are in me and I am in you, may they also be in us, so that the world may believe that you have sent me. The glory that you have given me I have given them, so that they may be one, as we are one, I in them and you in me, that they may become completely one, so the world may know that you have sent me and have loved them even as you have loved me.'

A Reading from the holy Gospel according to Matthew (5:13-16)

You are the salt of the earth but if salt has lost its taste how can its saltiness be restored? It is no longer good for anything but is thrown out and trampled underfoot. You are the light of the world. A city built on a hill cannot be hidden. No one after lighting a lamp puts in under the bushel basket but on the lampstand and it gives light to all in the house. In the same way, let your light shine before others so that they may see your good works and give glory to your Father in heaven.

A Reading from the holy Gospel according to Matthew (5:1-9)

When Jesus saw the crowds he went up the mountain and after he sat down his disciples came to him. Then he began to speak, and taught them, saying: 'Blessed are the poor in spirit, for theirs is the kingdom of heaven. Blessed are those who mourn, for they will be comforted. Blessed are the gentle, for they will inherit the earth. Blessed are those who hunger and thirst for righteousness, for they will be filled. Blessed are the merciful, for they will receive mercy. Blessed are the pure in heart, for they will see God. Blessed are the peacemakers, for they will be called children of God.'

A Reading from the holy Gospel according to Matthew (7:21)

Jesus said to his disciples: 'Not everyone who says to me "Lord, Lord", will enter the kingdom of heaven but only one who does the will of my Father in heaven. Everyone then who hears these words of mine and acts on them will be like a wise man who built his house on rock. The rain fell, the floods came and the winds blew and beat on that house, but it did not fall because it had been founded on rock. And everyone who hears these words of mine and does not act on them will be like a foolish man who built his house on sand. The rain fell and the floods came and the winds blew and beat against that house and it fell – and great was its fall!'

Now when Jesus had finished saying these things, the crowds were astonished at his teaching, for he taught them as one having authority and not as their scribes.

HOMILY

After the readings and the Gospel have been proclaimed, a homily is given. The purpose of this is to relate the content of the biblical passages to the life experience of the bride and groom, the chief witnesses and the entire congregation as the sacrament of marriage is celebrated. It is a reflection on the meaning of unconditional love, which is at the heart of the exchange of marriage vows.

THE RITE OF MARRIAGE

The chief witnesses (bride's maids and best/groom's man), if they have not already done so, join the bride and groom in the sanctuary of the church (at the altar). It is important that the bride and groom have a central position and are clearly visible to the whole congregation who, together with the presiding priest or deacon, are the Church before whom the couple exchange their consent.

There are four parts to the rite of marriage:

- Address to the couple;
- Exchange of consent or marriage vows;

- Blessing and exchange of rings; prayer of the newly married couple (optional);
- General intercessions or Prayers of the Faithful.

Each section offers a number of choices from which the couple may select when preparing the wedding liturgy. The priest/deacon and bride and groom may also make their own adaptation of what is given here.

Address

First Form

C.   Dear Children of God,

You have come today to pledge your love before God and before the Church here present in the person of the priest, your families and friends.

In becoming husband and wife you give yourselves to each other for life. You promise to be true and faithful, to support and cherish each other until death, so that your years together will be the living out in love of the pledge you now make.

May your love for each other reflect the enduring love of Christ for his Church. As you face the future together, keep in mind that the sacrament of marriage unites you with Christ and brings you, through the years, the grace and blessing of God our Father. Marriage is from God: he alone can give you the happiness which goes beyond human expectation and which grows deeper through the difficulties and struggles of life.

Put your trust in God as you set out together in life. Make your home a centre of Christian family life. (In this you will bequeath to your children a heritage more lasting than temporal wealth.)

The Christian home makes Christ and his Church present in the world of everyday things. May all who enter your home find there the presence of the Lord; for he has said: 'Where two or three are gathered together in my name, there am I in the midst of them.'

Now, as you are about to exchange your marriage vows the Church wishes to be assured that you appreciate the meaning of what you do, and so I ask you: Have you come here of your own free will and choice to marry each other?

Both   We have.

C.   Will you love and honour each other in marriage all the days of your life?

Both   We will.

C.   Are you willing to accept with love the children God may send you, and bring them up in accordance with the law of Christ, and his Church?

Both   We are.

Second Form

C.   Dear Children of God,

You have come to this Church so that the Lord may seal your love in the presence of the priest and this community.

Christian marriage is a sacred union which enriches natural love. It binds those who enter it to be faithful to each other for ever; it creates between them a bond that endures for life and cannot be broken; it demands that they love and honour each other (and that they accept from God the children he may give them, and bring them up in his love).

To help them in their marriage the husband and wife receive the life-long grace of the sacrament.

Is this your understanding of marriage?

Both   It is.

Third Form

C.   Dear Children of God,

You have come to this Church so that the Lord may seal your love in the presence of the priest and this community. Christ blesses this love. He has already consecrated you in baptism.

N. and N., you are about to celebrate this sacrament. Have you come here of your own free will and choice and without compulsion to marry each other?

Both   We have.

C.   Will you love and honour each other in marriage all the days of your life?

Both   We will.

The following question may be omitted if, for example, the couple is advanced in years.

C.   Are you willing to accept with love the children God may send you and bring them up in accordance with the law of Christ and his Church?

Both   We are.

Declaration of Consent

The priest/minister then invites the couple to declare their consent. He may use any of the six forms given below:

First Form

C.   I invite you then to declare before God and his Church your consent to become husband and wife.

G.   N., do you consent to be my wife?

B.   I do. Do you, N., consent to be my husband?

G.   I do.

G.   I take you as my wife and I give myself to you as your husband.

B.   I take you as my husband and I give myself to you as your wife.

They then join hands and say together:

To love each other truly
For better, for worse,
For richer, for poorer,
In sickness and in health,
Till death do us part. (OR all the days of our life.)

When the bride and groom have given their consent the priest says:

C.   What God joins together no one should separate.
May the Lord confirm the consent that you have given and enrich
you with his blessings.

Second Form

C.   I invite you then to declare before God and his Church your consent to become husband and wife.

They join hands.

G.   I, N., take you, N., as my wife,
       for better, for worse,
       for richer, for poorer,
       in sickness and in health,
       till death do us part. (OR all the days of our life.)

B.   I, N., take you, N., as my husband
       for better, for worse,
       for richer, for poorer,
       in sickness and in health,
       till death do us part. (OR all the days of our life.)

When the bride and groom have given their consent the priest/minister says:

C.   What God joins together no one should separate.
May the Lord confirm the consent that you have given and enrich
you with his blessings.

Third Form

C.   I invite you then to declare before God and his Church your consent to become husband and wife.

They join hands. The priest then asks the groom:

C.   N., do you take N. as your wife,
     for better, for worse,
     for richer, for poorer,
     in sickness and in health,
     till death do you part (OR all the rest of your life)?

G.   I do.

The priest then asks the bride:

C.   N., do you take N. as your husband,
     for better, for worse
     for richer, for poorer,
     in sickness and in health
     till death do you part (OR all the rest of your life)?

B.   I do.

C.   What God joins together no one should separate.
     May the Lord confirm the consent that you have given and enrich you with his blessings.

Fourth Form

C.   I invite you then to declare before God and his Church your decision to become husband and wife.

G.   N., do you consent to be my wife?

B.   I do.

B.   N., do you consent to be my husband?

G.   I do.

They join hands and say together:

Both   We take each other as husband and wife and promise to love each
       other truly,
       for better, for worse,
       for richer, for poorer,
       in sickness and in health,
       till death do us part. (OR all the days of our life.)

C.   The Lord has joined you together. May he fulfil his blessing in
       you; may he keep you in his love.

Fifth Form

C.   I invite you to declare before God and God's Church your consent
       to become husband and wife.

They join hands:

G.   I, N., take you, N., as my wife,
       for better, for worse,
       for richer, for poorer,
       in sickness and in health.
       I will love and cherish you
       all the days of my life.

B.   I, N., take you, N., as my husband,
       for better, for worse,
       for richer, for poorer,
       in sickness and in health.
       I will love and cherish you
       all the days of my life.

C.   You have declared your consent before the Church. May the Lord
       in his goodness strengthen your consent and fill you both with his
       blessing.

Sixth Form

G.   I, N., take you, N., as my wife,

in friendship and in love,
to have and to hold from this day forward.
I promise to be true to you
In good times and in bad,
in sickness and in health.
I will love you and cherish you all the days of my life.

B.   I, N., take you, N., as my husband,
in friendship and in love,
to have and to hold from this day forward.
I promise to be true to you,
in good times and in bad,
in sickness and in health.
I will love you and cherish you all the days of my life.

C.   The Lord has joined you together. May God fulfil his blessing in you; may he keep you in his love.

Blessing of Rings

First Form

C.   Lord, bless N. and N. and consecrate their married life.
May this ring (these rings) be a symbol of their faith in each other and a reminder of their love.
Through Christ our Lord.

Both   Amen.

Second Form

C.   May the Lord bless this ring (these rings) which will be the sign of your love and fidelity.

Both   Amen.

Third Form

C.   Lord, bless these rings.
Grant that those who wear them may always be faithful to each other.

May they do your will and live in peace with you in mutual love.
Through Christ our Lord.

Both   Amen.

Fourth Form

C.   Almighty God, bless this ring (these rings), symbols of faithfulness and unbroken love.
May N. and N. always be true to each other.
May they be one in heart and mind.
May they be united in love forever,
Through Christ our Lord.

Both   Amen.

The groom places a ring on the bride's finger. He may say:

G.   N., wear this ring as a sign of our faithful love (love and fidelity).
In the name of the Father and of the Son and of the Holy Spirit.

The bride may place a ring on the groom's finger. She may say:

B.   N., wear this ring as a sign of our faithful love (love and fidelity).
In the name of the Father and of the Son and of the Holy Spirit.

The groom may give gold and silver to the bride, saying:

G.   I give you this gold and silver, tokens of all I possess.

or

The bride and groom may exchange small symbolic gifts saying:

Both   N., I give you this gift, a token of all I possess.

C.   In the presence of God, and before this congregation, N. and N. have given their consent and made their marriage vows to each other. They have declared their marriage by the joining of hands and by the giving and receiving of a ring.

Therefore, in the name of God, I pronounce that they are husband and wife.

The couple are recommended to say together the following or some similar prayer:

We thank you, Lord
And we praise you
For bringing us
To this happy day.
You have given us to each other.
Now, together, we give ourselves to you.
We ask you, Lord:
Make us one in our love;
Keep us one in your peace.
Protect our marriage.
Bless our home.
Make us gentle.
Keep us faithful.
And when life is over
Unite us again
Where parting is no more
In the kingdom of your love.
There we will praise you
In the happiness and peace
Of our eternal home.
Amen.

Lighting of the Marriage Candle

Together the couple light a single candle from the two that were lit at the beginning of the Mass, as a symbol of their union as husband and wife.

Prayers of the Faithful

The following are sample Prayers of the Faithful from which you may choose a number to suit your needs:

C. God has given us the promise of fidelity and love in the Word of Scripture. N. and N. have given their promise of life-long faithful love in the Sacrament of Marriage. This hour of promise is also a time of prayer.
    We turn to God with confidence.

R. For our families, relatives and friends who walk with us on life's journey and especially for all those who have helped N. and N. reach this happy day.
    Lord hear us.
P. Lord graciously hear us.

R. That all Church leaders may be blessed in their efforts to make faith more relevant in the lives of people.
    Lord hear us.
P. Lord graciously hear us.

R. That all people in the world may experience justice and peace and especially that children may grow up in a peaceful and caring society.
    Lord hear us.
P. Lord graciously hear us.

R. For all who need our prayers and are in our thoughts today, that they may experience the caring presence of God in their lives.
    Lord hear us.
P. Lord graciously hear us.

R. For all who nurture young people and act as God's co-creators in developing their talents, that the fruits of their work may bring

variety, joy and inspiration to our lives.
Lord hear us.

P.   Lord graciously hear us.

R.   For those who have died, especially those whom we have known and loved, that they may enjoy perfect happiness and total fulfilment in eternal life.
Lord hear us.

P.   Lord graciously hear us.

R.   For the parents of N. and N., for their friends and all who have helped them to become husband and wife.
Lord hear us.

P.   Lord graciously hear us.

R.   We ask your blessing on all those who are here today; N. and N.'s parents, family members and friends, and on all who have guided them on their journey to this day.
Lord hear us.

P.   Lord graciously hear us.

R.   For our community and our families who welcome Christ into their lives; that they learn to receive him in the poor and suffering people of this world.
Lord hear us.

P.   Lord graciously hear us.

R.   For all who are victims of injustice and for those deprived of love and affection.
Lord hear us.

P.   Lord graciously hear us.

R. For married couples everywhere, that their lives will be an example to the world of unity, fidelity and love.
Lord hear us.

P. Lord graciously hear us.

R. For all couples preparing for marriage, and for those who are called to vocations other than marriage. May they find purpose and fulfilment in life and remain in your care.
Lord hear us.

P. Lord graciously hear us.

R. May the love of N. and N. be patient and gentle, ready to trust and endure whatever life brings. May their home be a gentle place of laughter, understanding and kindness.
Lord hear us.

P. Lord graciously hear us.

R. We pray especially today for N. and N., that the Lord who has brought them to this happy day will keep them forever in fidelity and love.
Lord hear us.

P. Lord graciously hear us.

R. For those who mourn while we are rejoicing, that in their suffering and loneliness they may experience the strength of God's support.
Lord hear us.

P. Lord graciously hear us.

R. While we are rejoicing we remember all those who are experiencing difficulties in their lives; the lonely, the sick, victims of injustice and all those deprived of love and affection.
Lord hear us.

P. Lord graciously hear us.

R.   We pray for the Church, the people of God, that we may know God's love for us and imitate that love in our love for one another and our respect for the earth which we inhabit.
Lord hear us.

P.   Lord graciously hear us.

R.   For the private intentions of all present, that God may grant whatever is for our good.
Lord hear us.

P.   Lord graciously hear us.

R.   That our relatives and friends who have made the passage through death may bask in the eternal light of God's love.
Lord hear us.

P.   Lord graciously hear us.

R.   For all our relatives and friends who have departed this life; may they remain in our thoughts and prayers and may God one day unite us again in eternity.
Lord hear us.

P.   Lord graciously hear us.

R.   May God guide N. and N. in their new life together and may they continue to live with respect, honour and love for each other.
Lord hear us.

P.   Lord graciously hear us.

R.   May God look kindly on N. and N. on this day of their marriage and provide them and all families with the grace and blessing that will enable them to continue to live out their life of love.
Lord hear us.

P.   Lord graciously hear us.

R.   For the parents of N. and N. who have provided them with support and unconditional love throughout their lives, and also for their friends and neighbours, who have watched them grow as individuals and as a couple over the years. May they continue to offer love and friendship as they begin their special journey today. Lord hear us.

P.   Lord graciously hear us.

R.   For absent relatives and friends who are unable to share in this happy occasion. We remember especially N. and N. whom we know are with us in spirit.
Lord hear us.

P.   Lord graciously hear us.

R.   For those who are victims of injustice across the world through famine, poverty and war, and for those deprived of love and affection. May the hearts of humankind be moved to promote God's reign of justice, love and peace.
Lord hear us.

P.   Lord graciously hear us.

C.   O ever-loving and caring God,
As we celebrate this sacramental moment in the lives of N. and N., we pray that their love may continue to deepen as they journey through life together.
We make these and all our prayers through Christ our Lord.

P.   Amen.

For an Inter-Church Wedding

C.   O ever-loving and caring God,
As we celebrate this sacramental moment in the lives of N. and N., we pray that the common threads of all Christian communities will weave into a blanket of God's love, covering all corners of the world.

PRAYER OVER THE GIFTS

The celebrant invites the people to pray:

C.   Pray my sisters and brothers that our sacrifice may be acceptable to God the almighty Father.

P.   May the Lord accept the sacrifice at your hands, for the praise and glory of God's name, for our good and the good of all God's Church.

The celebrant then says the prayer over the gifts. Any of the following three forms may be used:

C.   Lord,
Accept our offering for N. and N. By your love and providence you have brought them together. Now bless them all the days of their married life.
We ask this through Christ our Lord.

P.   Amen.

C.   Lord,
Accept the gifts we offer you on this happy day. In your fatherly love watch over and protect N. and N., whom you have united in marriage.
We ask this through Christ our Lord.

P.   Amen.

C.   Lord,
Hear our prayers and accept the gifts we offer for N. and N. Today you have made them one in the sacrament of marriage. May the mystery of Christ's unselfish love, which we celebrate in this Eucharist, increase their love for you and for each other.

P.   Amen.

THE EUCHARISTIC PRAYER

Any of the four eucharistic prayers may be used. Eucharistic Prayer 1 is given below, as it contains special forms:

C.   The Lord be with you.

P.   And also with you.

C.   Lift up your hearts.

P.   We lift them up to the Lord.

C.   Let us give thanks to the Lord our God.

P.   It is right to give him thanks and praise.

There are three special prefaces for marriage and normally one of these will be used:

Preface

C.   Father, all-powerful and ever-living God, we do well always and everywhere to give you thanks. By this sacrament your grace unites man and woman in an unbreakable bond of love and peace. You have designed the chaste love of husband and wife for the increase both of the human family and of your own family born in baptism. You are the loving Father of the world of nature; you are the loving Father of the new creation of grace. In Christian marriage you bring together the two orders of creation; nature's gift of children enriches the world and your grace enriches your Church. Through Christ, the choirs of angels and all the saints praise and worship your glory. May our voices blend with theirs as we join in their unending hymn of praise:

P.   Holy, holy, holy Lord, God of power and might, heaven and earth are full of your glory. Hosanna in the highest. Blessed is he who comes in the name of the Lord. Hosanna in the highest.

C.   Father, all-powerful and ever-living God, we do well always and everywhere to give you thanks through Jesus Christ our Lord. Through him you entered into a new covenant with your people. You restored us to grace in the saving mystery of redemption. You gave us a share in the divine life through our union with Christ. You made us the heirs of Christ's eternal glory. This outpouring of love in the new covenant of grace is symbolised in the marriage covenant that seals the love of husband and wife and reflects your divine plan of love. And so, with the angels and all the saints in heaven, we proclaim your glory and join in their unending hymn of praise:

P.   Holy, holy, holy Lord, God of power and might, heaven and earth are full of your glory. Hosanna in the highest. Blessed is he who comes in the name of the Lord. Hosanna in the highest.

C.   Father, all-powerful and ever-living God, we do well always and everywhere to give you thanks. You created us in love to share your divine life. We see our high destiny in the love of husband and wife, which bears the imprint of your own divine love. Love is our origin, love is our constant calling, love is our fulfilment in heaven. The love of man and woman is made holy in the sacrament of marriage and becomes the mirror of your everlasting love. Through Christ, the choirs of angels and all the saints praise and worship your glory. May our voices blend with theirs as we join in their unending hymn of praise:

P.   Holy, holy, holy Lord, God of power and might, heaven and earth are full of your glory. Hosanna in the highest. Blessed is he who comes in the name of the Lord. Hosanna in the highest.

First Eucharistic Prayer

C.   We come to you, Father, with praise and thanksgiving through Jesus Christ your Son. Through him we ask you to accept and bless these gifts we offer you in sacrifice. We offer them for your holy Catholic Church; watch over it, Lord, and guide it; grant it peace and unity throughout the world. We offer them for Benedict our Pope, for our Archbishop / Bishop and all the bishops, and for all who hold and teach the Catholic faith that comes to us from the apostles.

Remember Lord, your people, especially those for whom we now pray, N. and N. Remember all of us gathered here before you. You know how firmly we believe in you and dedicate ourselves to you. We offer you this sacrifice of praise for ourselves and those who are dear to us. We pray to you, our living and true God, for our well-being and redemption.

In union with the whole Church we honour Mary, the ever-virgin mother of Jesus Christ our Lord and God. We honour Joseph, her husband, the apostles and martyrs Peter and Paul, Andrew and all the saints.

May their merits and prayers gain us your constant help and protection. Father, accept this offering from your whole family and from N. and N., for whom we now pay. You have brought them to their wedding day: grant them (the gift and joy of children and) a long and happy life together.

Bless and approve our offering; make it acceptable to you, an offering in spirit and in truth. Let it become for us the body and blood of Jesus Christ, your only Son, our Lord.

The day before he suffered he took bread in his sacred hands and looking up to heaven, to you, his almighty Father, he gave you thanks and praise. He broke the bread, gave it to his disciples and said:

TAKE THIS, ALL OF YOU, AND EAT IT.

THIS IS MY BODY, WHICH WILL BE GIVEN UP FOR YOU.

When supper was ended he took the cup. Again he gave you thanks and praise, gave the cup to his disciples and said:

TAKE THIS, ALL OF YOU, AND DRINK FROM IT.

THIS IS THE CUP OF MY BLOOD,

THE BLOOD OF THE NEW AND EVERLASTING COVENANT.

IT WILL BE SHED FOR YOU AND FOR ALL
SO THAT SINS MAY BE FORGIVEN.
DO THIS IN MEMORY OF ME.

Let us proclaim the mystery of faith.

Memorial Acclamation of the People

P.   Christ has died,
Christ is risen,
Christ will come again.

C.   Father,
We celebrate the memory of Christ your Son. We, your people and your ministers, recall his passion, his resurrection from the dead and his ascension into glory; and from the many gifts you have given us we offer to you, God of glory and majesty, this holy and perfect sacrifice: the bread of life and the cup of eternal salvation.

Look with favour on these offerings and accept them as once you accepted the gifts of your servant Abel, the sacrifice of Abraham, our father in faith, and the bread and wine offered by your priest Melchisedech.

Almighty God, we pray that your angel may take this sacrifice to your altar in heaven. Then, as we receive from this altar the sacred body and blood of your Son, let us be filled with every grace and blessing.

Remember, Lord, those who have died and have gone before us marked with the sign of faith, especially those for whom we now pray, N. and N. May these, and all who sleep in Christ, find in your presence light, happiness and peace.

For ourselves too we ask some share in the fellowship of your apostles and martyrs, with John the Baptist, Stephen, Matthias, Barnabas and all the saints. Though we are sinners, we trust in your mercy and love. Do not consider what we truly deserve but grant us your forgiveness.

Through Christ our Lord you give us all these gifts. You fill them with life and goodness, you bless them and make them holy.

Through him,

with him,

in him,

in the unity of the Holy Spirit,

all glory and honour is yours, Almighty Father,

for ever and ever.

P.   Amen.

Second Eucharistic Prayer

C.   Lord, you are holy indeed, the fountain of all holiness.

Let your spirit come upon these gifts to make them holy so that they may become for us the body and blood of our Lord, Jesus Christ.

Before he was given up to death, a death he freely accepted, he took bread and gave you thanks. He broke the bread, gave it to his disciples and said:

TAKE THIS, ALL OF YOU, AND EAT IT.

THIS IS MY BODY, WHICH WILL BE GIVEN UP FOR YOU.

When supper was ended he took the cup. Again he gave you thanks and praise, gave the cup to his disciples and said:

TAKE THIS, ALL OF YOU, AND DRINK FROM IT.

THIS IS THE CUP OF MY BLOOD,

THE BLOOD OF THE NEW AND EVERLASTING COVENANT.

IT WILL BE SHED FOR YOU AND FOR ALL

SO THAT SINS MAY BE FORGIVEN.

DO THIS IN MEMORY OF ME.

Let us proclaim the mystery of faith.

Memorial Acclamation of the People

Choose one of the following:

P.   Christ has died,
     Christ is risen,
     Christ will come again.

P.   Dying you destroyed our death,
     Rising you restored our life.
     Lord Jesus, come in glory.

P.   When we eat this bread and drink this cup,
     We proclaim your death, Lord Jesus,
     Until you come in glory.

P.   Lord, by your cross and resurrection you have set us free.
     You are the Saviour of the world.

C.   In memory of his death and resurrection, we offer you, Father, this life-giving bread, this saving cup. We thank you for counting us worthy to stand in your presence and serve you.

     May all of us who share in the body and blood of Christ be brought together in unity by the Holy Spirit.

     Lord, remember your Church throughout the world. Make us grow in love, together with Benedict our Pope, our Archbishop/Bishop and all the clergy.

     Remember our sisters and brothers who have gone to their rest in the hope of rising again; bring them and all the departed into the light of your presence.

     Have mercy on us all; make us worthy to share eternal life

with Mary, the virgin mother of God, with the apostles and with all the saints who have done your will throughout the ages.

May we praise you in union with them and give you glory, through your Son, Jesus Christ.

Through him,

with him,

in him,

in the unity of the Holy Spirit,

all glory and honour is yours, Almighty Father,

for ever and ever.

P.   Amen.

Third Eucharistic Prayer

C.   Father,

You are holy indeed and all creation rightly gives you praise. All life, all holiness comes from you through your Son, Jesus Christ our Lord, by the working of the Holy Spirit. From age to age you gather your people to yourself, so that from east to west a perfect offering may be made to the glory of your name.

And so, Father, we bring you these gifts. We ask you to make them holy by the power of your Holy Spirit, so that they may become the body and blood of your Son, our Lord Jesus Christ, at whose command we celebrate this Eucharist.

On the night he was betrayed he took the bread and gave you thanks and praise. He broke the bread, gave it to his disciples and said:

TAKE THIS, ALL OF YOU, AND EAT IT.

THIS IS MY BODY, WHICH WILL BE GIVEN UP FOR YOU.

When supper was ended he took the cup. Again he gave you thanks and praise, gave the cup to his disciples and said:

TAKE THIS, ALL OF YOU, AND DRINK FROM IT.

THIS IS THE CUP OF MY BLOOD,

THE BLOOD OF THE NEW AND EVERLASTING COVENANT.

IT WILL BE SHED FOR YOU AND FOR ALL
SO THAT SINS MAY BE FORGIVEN.
DO THIS IN MEMORY OF ME.

Let us proclaim the mystery of faith.

Memorial Acclamation of the People
Choose one of the following:

P.   Christ has died,
Christ is risen,
Christ will come again.

P.   Dying you destroyed our death,
Rising you restored our life.
Lord Jesus, come in glory.

P.   When we eat this bread and drink this cup,
We proclaim your death, Lord Jesus,
Until you come in glory.

P.   Lord, by your cross and resurrection you have set us free.
You are the Saviour of the world.

C.   Father,
Calling to mind the death your Son endured for our salvation, his glorious resurrection and ascension into heaven, and ready to greet him when he comes again, we offer you in thanksgiving this holy and living sacrifice.

Look with favour on your Church's offering and see the victim whose death has reconciled us to yourself. Grant that we who are nourished by his body and blood may be filled with his Holy Spirit and become one body, one spirit, in Christ. May he make us an everlasting gift to you and enable us to share in the inheritance of your saints, with Mary, the virgin mother of God, with the apostles, the martyrs, Saint N. and all your saints on whose constant intercession we rely for help.

Lord, may this sacrifice, which has made our peace with you, advance the peace and salvation of all the world. Strengthen in faith and love your pilgrim Church on earth, your servant Pope Benedict, our Archbishop/Bishop and all the bishops, with the clergy and the entire people your Son has gained for you.

Father, hear the prayers of the family you have gathered here before you. In mercy and love unite all your children wherever they may be. Welcome into your kingdom our departed brothers and sisters and all who have left this world in your friendship.

We hope to enjoy for ever the vision of your glory, through Christ our Lord from whom all good things come.
Through him,
with him,
in him,
in the unity of the Holy Spirit,
all glory and honour is yours, Almighty Father,
For ever and ever.

P.   Amen.

Fourth Eucharistic Prayer

C.   Father,
We acknowledge your greatness: all your actions show your wisdom and love.

You formed us in your own likeness and set us over the whole world to serve you, our creator, and to rule over all creatures. Even when we disobeyed you and lost your friendship you did not abandon us to the power of death, but helped all to seek and find you. Again and again you offered a covenant to us and through the prophets taught us to hope for salvation.

Father, you so loved the world that in the fullness of time you sent your only Son to be our Saviour. He was conceived through the power of the Holy Spirit and born of the Virgin Mary, a man like us in all things but sin. To the poor he proclaimed the good news of salvation, to prisoners, freedom, and to those in sorrow, joy.

In fulfilment of your will he gave himself up to death; but by rising from the dead he destroyed death and restored life. And that we might live no longer for ourselves but for him he sent the Holy Spirit from you, Father, as his first gift to those who believe, to complete his work on earth and bring us the fullness of grace.

Father, may this Holy Spirit sanctify these offerings. Let them become the body and blood of Jesus Christ our Lord as we celebrate the great mystery which he left us as an everlasting covenant.

He always loved those who were his own in the world.

When the time came for him to be glorified by you, his heavenly Father, he showed the depth of his love.

While they were at supper, he took bread, said the blessing, broke the bread and gave it this disciples, saying:

TAKE THIS, ALL OF YOU, AND EAT IT.

THIS IS MY BODY, WHICH WILL BE GIVEN UP FOR YOU.

In the same way, he took the cup, filled with wine. He gave you thanks, and giving the cup to his disciples, said:

TAKE THIS, ALL OF YOU, AND DRINK FROM IT.

THIS IS THE CUP OF MY BLOOD,

THE BLOOD OF THE NEW AND EVERLASTING COVENANT.

IT WILL BE SHED FOR YOU AND FOR ALL

SO THAT SINS MAY BE FORGIVEN.

DO THIS IN MEMORY OF ME.

Let us proclaim the mystery of faith.

Memorial Acclamation of the People
Choose one of the following:

P.   Christ has died,
      Christ is risen,
      Christ will come again.

P.   Dying you destroyed our death,
      Rising you restored our life.
      Lord Jesus, come in glory.

P.   When we eat this bread and drink this cup,
      We proclaim your death, Lord Jesus,
      Until you come in glory.

P.   Lord, By your cross and resurrection you have set us free.
      You are the Saviour of the world.

C.   Father,
      We now celebrate this memorial of our redemption.
      We recall Christ's death, his descent among the dead, his resur-
      rection and his ascension to your right hand; and looking for-
      ward to his coming in glory we offer you his body and blood,
      the acceptable sacrifice which brings salvation to the whole
      world.

         Lord, look upon this sacrifice which you have given to your
      Church and by your Holy Spirit, gather all who share this bread
      and wine into the one body of Christ, a living sacrifice of
      praise.

         Lord, remember those for whom we offer this sacrifice, espe-
      cially Benedict our Pope, our Archbishop/Bishop and bishops
      and clergy everywhere.

Remember those who take part in this offering, those here present and all your people, and all who seek you with a sincere heart.

Remember those who have died in the peace of Christ and all the dead whose faith is known to you alone.

Father, in your mercy grant also to us, your children, to enter into our heavenly inheritance in the company of the Virgin Mary, the Mother of God, and your apostles and saints.

Then, in your kingdom, freed from the corruption of sin and death we shall sing your glory with every creature through Christ our Lord, through whom you give us everything that is good.
Through him,
with him,
in him,
in the unity of the holy spirit, all glory and honour is yours, Almighty Father,
for ever and ever.

P.   Amen.

Communion Rite

The Lord's Prayer

C.   Let us pray with confidence to the Father in the words our Saviour gave us:

All   Our Father, who art in heaven,
        hallowed be thy name.
        Thy kingdom come.
        Thy will be done on earth, as it is in heaven.
        Give us this day our daily bread,
        and forgive us our trespasses,
        as we forgive those who trespass against us,
        and lead us not into temptation,
        but deliver us from evil.

NUPTIAL BLESSING

Immediately after the Lord's Prayer the celebrant faces the bride and groom and blesses them, using one of the following four forms (words in brackets may be omitted):

C.   Let us ask God to bless N. and N., now married in Christ, and unite them in his love (through the sacrament of his body and blood).

Silent prayer. Then the celebrant continues:

C.   God, our Father, creator of the universe, you made man and woman in your own likeness and blessed their union. We humbly pray to you for this groom and bride, today united in the sacrament of marriage.

May your blessing come upon them. May they find happiness in their love for each other (be blessed in their children) and enrich the life of the Church.

May they praise you in their days of happiness and turn to you in times of sorrow.

May they know the joy of your help in their work and the strength of your presence in their need. May they worship you with the Church and be your witnesses in the world. May old age come to them in the company of their friends and may they reach at last the kingdom of heaven.

We ask this through Christ our Lord.

P.   Amen.

C.   Let us ask God to bless N. and N., now married in Christ, and unite them in his love.

Silent payer. Then the celebrant continues:

C.   Father, you created the universe and made man and woman in your own likeness. You gave woman as companion to man so that they should no longer be two, but one flesh, teaching us that those you have so united may never be separated.

       Father, you have sanctified marriage in a mystery so holy that it is a sign of the union of Christ and his Church. Look with love upon N. as she asks your blessing. May she live in peace with you and follow the example of those women whose lives are praised in the scriptures. May N. place his trust in her and see her as his companion. May he always honour her and love her as Christ loves the Church.

       Father, keep this husband and wife strong in faith and true to your commandments. May they be faithful to each other, examples of Christian living and witnesses of Christ. (Bless them with children and help them to be good parents.) And after a long and happy life together may they enjoy the company of your saints in heaven.

       We ask this through Christ our Lord.

P.   Amen.

C.   Let us pray to the Lord for N. and N., who as they begin their married life come to God's altar to deepen their love (by sharing in the body and blood of Christ).

Silent prayer. Then the celebrant continues:

C.   Father, you created man and woman in your own image and united them in body and heart so that they might fulfil your plan for the world. To reveal your loving design, you made the union of husband and wife a sign of the covenant between you and your people; through the sacrament of marriage you perfect this union and make it now a sign of Christ's love for his bride, the Church.

       Lord, bless this husband and wife and protect them. Grant that as they live this sacrament they may learn to share with each other the gifts of your love. May they become one in heart and mind as witnesses to your presence in their marriage. (Bless them with children who will be formed by the gospel and have a place in your family in heaven.)

May N. be a good wife (and mother), caring for her home, faithful to her husband, generous and kind.

May N. be a good husband (and a devoted father), gentle and strong, faithful to his wife and a careful provider for his household.

Father, grant that, as they now come as husband and wife to your altar, they may one day share your feast in heaven.

We ask this through Christ our Lord.

P. Amen.

C. We call God our Father. Let each of us now ask him, in silence, to bless these his children as they begin their married life.

Silent prayer. Then the celebrant continues:

C. Father, from you every family in heaven and earth takes its name. You made us. You made all that exists. You made man and woman like yourself in their power to know and love. You call them to share life with each other, saying, 'It is not good for man or woman to be alone'. (You bless them with children to give new life to your people, telling them, 'Increase and multiply, and fill the earth'.)

We call to mind the fruitful companionship of Abraham, our father in faith, and his wife, Sarah. We remember how your guiding hand brought Rebecca and Isaac together, and how through the lives of Jacob and Rachel you prepared the way for God's reign.

Father, you take delight in the love of husband and wife, that love which hopes and shares, heals and forgives. We ask you to bless N. and N. as they set out on their new life. Fill their hearts with your Holy Spirit, the spirit of understanding, joy, fortitude and peace. Strengthen them to do your will and in the trials of life to bear the cross with Christ. May they praise you during the bright days and call on you in times of trouble. (May their children bring them your blessing, and give glory to your name.) Let their love be strong as death, a fire that floods cannot drown, a jewel beyond all price. May their life together give witness to their faith in Christ. May they see long and happy days and be united forever in the kingdom of your glory.

    We ask this through Christ our Lord.

P.   Amen.

Silent prayer. The celebrant continues:

C.   Lord Jesus Christ, you said to your apostles: I leave you peace, my peace I give you. Look not on our sins, but on the faith of your Church, and grant us the peace and unity of your kingdom where you live for ever and ever.

P.   Amen.

C.   The peace of the Lord be with you always.

P.   And also with you.

The celebrant may then say:

C.   Let us offer each other the sign of peace.

P.   Lamb of God, you take away the sins of the world:
have mercy on us.
Lamb of God, you take away the sins of the world:
have mercy on us.
Lamb of God, you take away the sins of the world:
grant us peace.

The celebrant then invites the people to communion.

C.   This is the Lamb of God who takes away the sins of the world. Happy are those who are called to his table.

P.   Lord, I am not worthy to receive you, but only say the word and I shall be healed.

The communion now follows. The bride and groom, bridal party and indeed the whole congregation may receive communion under both kinds.

Communion Reflection

One of the following Communion Reflections may be used:

Reflection I

You are a man and woman of love. You bring to this wedding ceremony all that you are and all that has made you who you are: your families, your friends, your giftedness, your experience of life, your insights, and your wisdom. You bring your hopes and your dreams of what shared love might be.

In your love for each other we see the Spirit of Love and Life in human form and we rejoice in the wonderful ways each of you makes that Spirit visible to us. Be always the man and woman you are because that is what delights and attracts you and brings you together. It is also what we, your family and friends, delight in. But let there also be space and room for the other to grow as you form a bond this day that you may wish to be unending and unbreakable. May that bonding be joyful and gracious. May your love be overflowing and generous.

In all the years to come may you delightedly be N. and N., wife and husband, strong and constant in love for each other, for your families and for your friends.

Michael Morwood, *Praying a New Story*

Reflection 2

Masons, when they start upon a building,
are careful to test the scaffolding:
make sure that planks won't slip at busy points,
secure all ladders, tighten bolted joints.
And yet all this comes down, when the job's done,
showing off walls of sure and solid stone.
So if, my dear, there sometimes seem to be
old bridges breaking between you and me,
never fear. We may have let the scaffolds fall,
confident that we have built our wall.

Seamus Heaney, 'Scaffolding'

Reflection 3

Now you feel no rain,
for each of you will be a shelter to the other.
Now you feel no cold,
for each of you will be warmth to the other.
Now there is no loneliness,
for each of you will be a companion to the other.
You are two bodies,
but there is one life before you and one home.
When evening falls,
each will look up and the other will be there.
He'll take her hand; she will take his
and you'll turn together
To look at the road you travelled to reach this:
the hour of your happiness.
It stretches behind you, even as the future lies ahead,
a long and winding road, whose every turning
means discovery.
Old hopes, new laughter, shared fears.
Your adventure has just begun.

'The Apache Wedding Blessing'

Reflection 4

God in heaven above, please protect the ones we love.
We honour all you created as we pledge our hearts and lives together.
We honour Mother Earth and ask for our marriage to be abundant and grow stronger through the seasons.
We honour fire and ask that our union be warm and glowing with love in our hearts.
We honour wind and ask that we sail through life safe and calm as in our father's arms – that it may never thirst for love.
We honour water, to clean and soothe our marriage – that it may never thirst for love.
All the forces of the universe you created, we pray for harmony and true happiness as we forever grow young together.
Amen.

'Cherokee Prayer'

Reflection 5

If two are caring as they are sharing life's hopes and fears;
If music of laughter outweighs sadness and tears;
Marriage is togetherness.
If both derive pleasure from the mere presence of each other;
Yet when parted no jealousies restrict, worry or smother;
Marriage is freedom.
If achievements mean more when they benefit two;
And consideration is shown with each point of view;
Marriage is respect.
And if togetherness, freedom and respect are combined with a joy that words can never fully define, then marriage is love.

'Marriage Is Love'

Reflection 6

If you can always be as close and happy as today
Yet be secure enough to grow and change along the way.
If you can keep for you alone your love as man and wife

Yet find the time to share your joy with others in your life.
If you can be as one and walk through marriage hand in hand,
Yet still support the goals and dreams that each of you have planned.
If you can dare to always go your separate ways together;
Then all the wonder of today will stay with you forever.
Always love each other.
And keep close to your heart the plans you've made
And the dreams you've seen come true.
Keep close to your heart the loving things each of you say and do.
Keep close to your heart
The memories of the happy times you've known
The caring and understanding times
And the way your love has grown.
And may you both treasure all these things, for they're such a special part of your union today, with the one you love, who will always be close to your heart.

Reflection 7

Then Almitra spoke again and said, 'and what of marriage, master?'
And he answered saying:
'You were born together and together you shall be forevermore.
You shall be together when white wings of death scatter your days.
Aye, you shall be together even in the silent memory of God.
But let there be spaces in your togetherness,
and let the winds of the heavens dance between you.
Love one another but make not a bond of love:
Let it rather be a moving sea between the shores of your souls.
Fill each other's cup but drink not from one cup.
Give one another of your bread but eat not from the same loaf.
Sing and dance together and be joyous, but let each one of you be alone, even as the strings of the lute are alone although they quiver with the same music.
Give your hearts but not into each other's keeping,
for only the hand of Life can contain your hearts,

and stand together yet not too near together:
for the pillars of the temple stand apart, and the oak tree and the cypress
grow not in each other's shadow.

> Kahlil Gibran (1883–1931), *The Prophet*

Reflection 8

When we love, we see things other people do not see.
We see beneath the surface to the qualities which make our beloved special and unique.
To see with loving eyes is to know inner beauty.
And to be loved is to be seen and known as we are known to no other.
One who loves us gives us a unique gift;
A piece of ourselves, but a piece that only they could give us.
We who love can look at each other's life and say,
'I touched his life' or 'I touched her life'
just as an artist might say 'I touched this canvas'.
'Those brushstrokes in the corner of this magnificent mural, those are mine.'
'I was part of this life and it is a part of me.'
Marriage is to belong to each other through a unique and diverse collaboration,
like two threads crossing in different directions, yet weaving one tapestry together.

> Author unknown, 'So What Do We Mean by Love?'

Reflection 9

Love is a temporary madness,
it erupts like volcanoes and then subsides,
and when it subsides you have to make a decision.
You have to work out whether your roots have so entwined together
that it is inconceivable that you should ever part.
Because this is what love is.
Love is not breathlessness.

It is not excitement.
It is not the promulgation of eternal passion.
That is just being 'in love' which any fool can do.
Love itself is what is left over when being in love has burned away
and this is both an art and a fortunate accident.
Those that truly love have roots that grow towards each other under-
ground and when all the pretty blossom has fallen from their branches
they find that they are one tree and not two.

Louis de Berniere, Captain Corelli's Mandolin

Reflection 10

The love of God, unutterable and perfect,
flows into a pure soul the way that light
rushes into a transparent object.
The more love that it finds, the more it gives itself;
so that as we grow clear and open,
the more complete the joy of loving is,
and the more souls who resonate together, the greater the intensity of
their love,
For, mirror-like, each soul reflects the other.

Dante (1265–1321), 'The Divine Comedy'

Reflection 11

When two people are at one in their inmost hearts
they shatter even the strength of iron or of bronze
and when two people understand each other in their inmost hearts
their words are sweet and strong like the fragrance of orchids.

The I Ching (c.1000 BC), 'When Two People are at One'

Reflection 12

How do I love thee? Let me count the ways.
I love thee to the depth and breadth and height
my soul can reach, when feeling out of sight

for the ends of Being and ideal Grace.
I love thee to the level of every day's
most quiet need, by sun and candle-light.
I love thee freely, as men strive for Right;
I love thee purely, as they turn from Praise.
I love thee with the passion put to use
in my old griefs, and with my childhood's faith:
I love thee with a love I seemed to lose
with my lost saints – I love thee with the breath,
smiles, tears of all my life! – and, if God choose,
I shall but love thee better after death.

> Elizabeth Barrett Browning (1806–1861), 'Sonnets from the Portuguese'

Reflection 13

A good marriage must be created.
In a marriage the little things are the big things.
It is never being too old to hold hands.
It is remembering to say 'I love you' at least once a day.
It is never going to sleep angry.
It is at no time taking the other for granted.
The courtship should not end with the honeymoon.
It should continue through all the years.
It is having a mutual sense of values and common objectives.
It is a standing together facing the world.
It is forming a circle of love that gathers in the whole family.
It is doing things for each other, not in the attitude of duty or sacrifice, but in the spirit of joy.
It is speaking words of appreciation and demonstrating gratitude in thoughtful ways.
It is not expecting the husband to wear a halo or the wife the wings of an angel.
It is not looking for perfection in each other.

It is cultivating flexibility, patience, understanding and a sense of humour.
It is having the capacity to forgive and forget.
It is giving each other an atmosphere in which each can grow.
It is finding room for the things of the spirit.
It is a common search for the good and the beautiful.
It is establishing a relationship in which the independence is equal, dependence is mutual and the obligation is reciprocal.
It is not only marrying the right partner.
It is being the right partner.

Wilfred A. Peterson, 'Art of Marriage'

Reflection 14

We shall not cease from exploration
and the end of all our exploring
will be to arrive where we started
and to know the place for the first time.
Through the unknown, remembered gate
when the last of earth left to discover
is that which was the beginning;
at the source of the longest river
the voice of the hidden waterfall
and the children in the apple tree
not known, because not looked for
but heard, half-heard, in the stillness
between two waves of the sea.
Quick now, here, now, always –
a condition of complete simplicity.

Author unknown

Reflection 15

I love you not only for what you are
but for what I am when I am with you.
I love you not only for what you have made of yourself,

but for what you are making of me.
I love you for the part of me that you bring out;
I love you for putting your hand into my heaped-up heart
and passing over all the foolish weak things
that you can't help dimly seeing there
and for drawing out into the light all the beautiful belongings
that no one else had looked quite far enough to find.
I love you because you are helping me to make of the lumber of my life
not a tavern but a temple;
out of the works of my every day not a reproach but a song.
I love you because you have done more
than any creed could have done to make me good
and more than any fate could have done to make me happy.
You have done it without a word, without a sign.
You have done it by being yourself.
Perhaps that is what being a friend means after all.
   Roy Croft (1907–1973), 'I Love You'

Reflection 16

Across the years I will walk with you,
in deep green forests;
on shores of sand;
and when our time on earth is through
in heaven too,
you will have my hand.
   Author unknown

Reflection 17

Let me not to the marriage of true minds
admit impediments; love is not love
which alters when it alteration finds,
or bends with the remover to remove.
O, no, it is an ever-fixed mark,
that looks on tempests and is never shaken;

it is the star to every wand'ring bark,
whose worth's unknown, although his height be taken.
Love's not time's fool, though rosy lips and cheeks
within his ending sickle's compass come;
love alters not with his brief hours and weeks,
but bears it out even to the edge of doom.
If this be error and upon me proved,
I never writ, nor no man ever loved.

William Shakespeare (1564–1616), Sonnet 116

Reflection 18

No speed of wind or water rushing by
but you have speed far greater. You can climb
back up a steam of radiance to the sky,
and back through history up the stream of time.
And you were given this swiftness, not for haste,
nor chiefly that you may go where you will, but in the rush of everything
to waste,
that you may have the power of standing still –
off any still or moving thing you say.
Two such as you with such a master speed
cannot be parted nor be swept away
from one another once you are agreed
that life is only life forevermore
together wing to wing and oar to oar.

Robert Frost (1874–1963), 'The Master Speed'

Reflection 19

O my luve's like a red, red rose,
that's newly sprung in June;
sweetly play'd in tune.
As fair art thou, my bonnie lass,
so deep in luve am I,

and I will luve thee still, my Dear,
till a' the seas gang dry.
Til a' the seas gang dry, my Dear,
and the rocks melt wi' the sun!
And I will luve thee still my Dear,
while the sands o' life shall run.

> Robert Burns (1759–1796), 'A Red, Red Rose'

Reflection 20

I cannot promise you a life of sunshine;
I cannot promise riches, wealth or gold;
I cannot promise you an easy pathway
that leads away from change or growing old.
But I can promise all my heart's devotion,
a smile to chase away your tears of sorrow;
a love that's ever true and ever growing;
a hand to hold in yours through each tomorrow.

> Mark Twain (1835–1910), 'These I Can Promise'

Reflection 21

Had I the heavens' embroidered cloths,
enwrought with golden and silver light,
the blue and the dim and the dark cloths
of night and light and the half-light,
I would spread the cloths under your feet:
But I, being poor, have only my dreams;
I have spread my dreams under your feet;
Tread softly because you tread on my dreams.

> W.B. Yeats (1965–1939), 'He Wishes for the Cloths of Heaven'

Reflection 22

I wonder, by my troth, what thou and I
did, till we loved? Were we not weaned till then?

But sucked on country pleasures, childishly?
Or stored we in the seven sleepers' den?
'Twas so; but this, all pleasures fancies be.
If ever any beauty I did see,
which I desired, and got, 'twas but a dream of thee.
And now good-morrow to our waking souls,
which watch not one another out of fear;
for love, all love of other sights controls
and makes one little room, an everywhere.
Let sea-discoverers to new worlds have gone,
let maps to others, worlds on worlds have shown,
let us possess one world, each hath one, and is one.
My face in thine eye, thine in mine appears,
And true plain hearts do in the faces rest;
where can we find two better hemispheres,
without sharp North, without declining West?
Whatever dies, was not mixed equally;
if our two loves be one, or, thou and I
Love so alike, that none do slacken, none can die.

John Donne (1572–1631), 'The Good-Morrow'

Reflection 23

Love is enough: though the World be a-waning,
and the woods have no voice but the voice of complaining,
though the sky be too dark for dim eyes to discover
the gold-cups and daisies fair blooming thereunder,
though the hills be held shadows, and the sea a dark wonder,
and this day draw a veil over all deeds pass'd over,
yet their hands shall not tremble, their feet shall not falter;
the void shall not weary, the fear shall not alter
these lips and these eyes of the loved and the lover.

William Morris (1834–1896), 'Love is Enough'

Reflection 24

That is the true season of love, when we believe that we alone can love, that no one could ever have loved so before us, and that no one will ever love in the same way after us.

> Johann Wolfgang von Goethe (1749–1832), 'That is the True Season of Love'

Reflection 25

The spring comes in with all her hues and smells,
a freshness breathing over hills and dells;
o'er woods where May her gorgeous drapery flings,
and meads washed fragrant untouched and free
from the bold rifling of the amorous bee.
The happy time of singing birds is come,
and love's lone pilgrimage now finds a home;
amongst the mossy oaks now coos the dove,
and the hoarse crow finds softer notes for love.
The foxes play around their dens, and bark
in joy's excess, 'mid woodland shadows dark;
the flowers join lips below; the leaves above;
and every sound that meets the ear is love.

> John Clare (1793–1864), 'A Spring Morning'

Reflection 26

May the road rise to meet you.
May the wind be always at your back.
May the sun shine warm upon your face,
the rains fall soft upon your fields
and until we meet again
may God hold you in the palm of his hand.
May God be with you and bless you.
May you see your children's children.
May you be poor in misfortune,
rich in blessings.

May you know nothing but happiness
from this day forward.
May the road rise to meet you.
May the wind be always at your back.
May the warm rays of sun fall upon your home
and may the hand of a friend always be near.
May green be the grass you walk on.
May blue be the skies above you.
May pure be the joys that surround you.
May true be the hearts that love you.

Author unknown, Traditional Irish Blessing

Reflection 27

Make our hands one hand
Make our hearts one heart
Make our vows one vow.
Only death can part us now.
Make our life one life.
Day after day only life,
Now we begin, now we start.
One hand, one heart.
Even death won't part us now.

Author unknown

PRAYER AFTER COMMUNION

C.   Let us pray.

The celebrant and people pray silently for a while. Then the celebrant says the prayer after communion. Any of the following forms may be used:

C.   Lord,

In your love you have given us this Eucharist to unite us with one another and with you. As you have made N. and N. one in this sacrament of marriage (and in the sharing of the one bread and the one cup), so now make them one in love for each other.

We ask this through Christ our Lord.

P.   Amen.

C.   Lord,

We who have shared the food of your table pray for our friends N. and N, whom you have joined together in marriage.

Keep them close to you always.

May their love for each other proclaim to all the world their faith in you.

We ask this through Christ our Lord.

P.   Amen.

C.   Almighty God,

May the sacrifice we have offered and the Eucharist we have shared strengthen the love of N. and N., and give us all your fatherly aid.

We ask this through Christ our Lord.

R.   Amen.

CONCLUDING RITE

C.   The Lord be with you.

P.   And also with you.

The celebrant first blesses the bride and groom and then blesses all present. One of the following forms may be used:

C. May God, the eternal Father, keep you steadfast in your love.

P. Amen.

C. May you have children to bless you, friends to console you and may you live in peace with all.

P. Amen.

C. May you bear witness among all to the love of God.
May the suffering and the poor find you generous and welcome you one day into our Father's kingdom.

P. Amen.

C. May the peace of Christ ever dwell in your home. May the angels of God protect it and may the holy family of Nazareth be its model and inspiration.

P. Amen.

C. May God, the almighty Father, grant you his joy.
May he bless you in your children.

P. Amen.

C. May Jesus Christ, the Son of God, in his mercy help you in good times and in bad.

P. Amen.

C. May the Holy Spirit of God always fill you with his love.

P. Amen.

C. The Lord Jesus was present at the wedding in Cana; today may he bless you and your families and friends.

P. Amen.

C. He loved his Church to the end;
may he fill your hearts to overflowing with his love.

P. Amen.

C. May he give you the grace to bear witness to his resurrection, and look forward to his coming with hope and joy.

P. Amen.

C.   May the peace of Christ ever dwell in your home;
       may the angels of God protect it,
       and may the holy family of Nazareth
       be its model and inspiration.

P.   Amen.

God of love and life, out of this world two souls have found each other.
Their destinies shall now be woven into one design and their joys shall
not be known apart. N. and N., may your home be a place of happiness
for all who enter it, a place where the old and the young are renewed in
each other's company, a place for growing and a place for sharing, a place
for music and a place for laughter, a place for prayer and a place for love.
May those who are nearest to you be constantly enriched by the beauty
and the bounty of your love for one another. May your work be a joy of
your life that serves the world and may your days be good and long upon
the earth.

BLESSING AND DISMISSAL

C.   May almighty God bless you all, the Father, the Son and the Holy
       Spirit.

P.   Amen.

C.   Let us go from here in peace and in love to continue our celebra-
       tion.

P.   Thanks be to God.

CONCLUSION

I trust that you have found the content of this book easy to follow and that you have been able to choose the readings, prayers, form of marriage vows, nuptial blessings and reflections to match your experience of life and love as a unique couple.

In working with couples in preparation for their wedding liturgy I have noticed that the more thought, consideration and time that is given to this, the more meaningful and beautiful the ceremony is on the day.

I wish all those who use this book many years of happiness in their married life.

APPENDIX

THE RITE OF MARRIAGE IN THE IRISH LANGUAGE

GAIRMGHLAOCH

S.   Bíodh a fhios agaibh go bhfuilimid bailithe anseo.
chun glacadh le rún pósta A. agus A.
chun aontachta agus aontíos;
chun grá agus dílseachta;
chun measa agus onóra;
chun carthanachta agus measarthachta;
chun misnight agus féile;
chun móraigheantachta agus maithiúnais;
chun buaine go bás.
I láthair Dé agus na hEaglaise,
in ainm na Tríonóide RóNaofa
agus í síocháin na Páise;
in onóir na Maighdine Muire, Máthair Dé,
na Naomh Aspal agus na Naomh uile;
faoi bhrí na Sacriminte Naofa;
iarraim oraibh an bhfuil sibh toilteanach
glacadh lena chéile mar fhear agus mar bhean chéile?
Lanuin; Táimid toilteanach.

(S. An nglachfaidh sibh le cibé leanaí a churifidh
Dia chugaibh an dtógfaidh sibh aid de réir dhlí Chríost agus na hEaglaise?
Lanuin: Glacfaimid agus tógfaimid.)

DEARBHU TOILTEANAIS

S.   Tugaim cuireadh daoibh dearbhú os conhair Dé agus na hEaglaise gurb é bhur dtoil é go ndéanfaí fear céile agus bean chéile díbh.

Beieann siad greim laimhe ar a chéile. Deir an fear:

F.   Glacaimse, A., leatsa, a A., mar bhean chéile,
más fearr sin, más measa,
más tinn nó mas slán
go scara an bás sinn. (Nó ach lá dár saol.)

Deir an bhrideog:

B.   Glacaimse A., leatsa a A., mar flear chéile,
más fearr sin, más measa,
más tinn nó más slán,
go scara an bás sinn. (Nó gach lá dár saol.)

Tar éis don lánúin a dtoil dá chéile a chur in iúl, deir an sagart:

S.   An ní a cheanglaíonn Dia, ná scaoileadh duine é.
Go neartaí Dia leis an toil atá tugtha agaibh dá chéile
agus go mbronna sé a bheannacht oraibh go fial.

BEANNU NA bhFAINNI

S.   Beannaigh A., agus A., a Thiarna, agus déan a saol pósta a choiscreacan.
Go raibh an fáinne (na fáinní) seo mar chomhartha ar a ndílseacht agus go gcuire sé (said) i gcuimhne dóibh a ngrá da chéile.
Sin é ar nguí chugat trí Chríost ár dTiarna.

Pobal: Amen.

Croitheann an sagart uisce coisrichte ar na fainni.
Cuireann an fear fainne na mna ar a fainneog. Ni miste do a ra:

F.   AA., caith an fáinne seo mar chomhartha ar ár ngrá
       agus ar ár ndílseacht.
       In ainm an Athar agus an Mhic agus an Spioraid Naoimh.
       Amen.

Ní miste don bhrídeog fáinne an fhir a chur ar fháinneog siúd.
Ní miste di a rá:

B.   AA., caith an fáinne seo mar chomhartha an ár ngrá
       agus ar ár ndílseacth.

In ainm an Athar agus an Mhic agus an Spioraid Naoimh. Amen.

AN TABHARTAS

Ní miste don fhear ór agus airgead a thabhairt dá bhean chéile, á rá:

F.   Tugaim duit an t-ór agus an t-airgead seo,
       comhartaí ar mo mhaoin shaolta uile.

Nó ní miste don fhear agus don bhrídeog bronntanais bheaga
shiombalacha a thabhairt dá chéile, á rá:

F.   AA., tugaim an bronntanas seo duit, i ngeall ar mo mhaoinn
       shaolta uile.

Guí an Phobail (An ceann seo nó ceann eile)

S: Guímis: Ag an bpósadh a bhí i Cána bhí Rí na nGrás ann i bpearsa. Iarraimis air an lánúin seo a bheannú, faoi mar a bheannaigh sé an bhainis úd i nGailile.

B: A Íosa, a Mhic Muire,
Déan trócaire orainn.

P: A Rí na Rí,
A Dhia na nDúl.

F: Bí um thús ár slí,
Bí um chríoch ár saoil.

P: A Rí na Rí,
A Dhia na nDúl.

B: Bí ag múscailt ár mbeatha,
Bí ag dubhadh ár lae.

P: A Rí na Rí,
A Dhia na nDúl.

F: Bí romhainn agus linn,
Go deireadh ár ré.

P: A Rí na Rí,
A Dhia na nDúl.

B: Coisric sinn,
Croí agus crann.

P: A Rí na Rí,
A Dhia na nDúl.

F: Coisric sinn,
          Corp agus cuid.

P: A Rí na Rí,
          A Dhia na nDúl.

B: Coisric sinn,
          Croí agus cré.

P: A Rí na Rí,
          A Dhia na nDúl.

F: Ár gcroí is ár gcré,
          Gach lá duit féin.

P: A Rí na Rí,
          A Dhia na nDúl.

Athair na Brídeoige:
          Bua ratha daoibh:
          Bua mac is iníonacha daoibh:
          Bua mara is tíre daoibh.

Máthair na Brídeoige:
          Bua grá daoibh:
          Bua dílse daoibh:
          Bua Flaithis daoibh:
          Bua lae is oíche daoibh.

Athair an Fhir:
          Maitheas mara daoibh:
          Maitheas talaimh daoibh:
          Maitheas Neimhe daoibh.

Máthair an Fhir:
> Gach lá sona daoibh:
> Gan lá dona daoibh:
> Onóir is urraim daoibh:
> Grá gach duine daoibh.

S: A Dhia shíoraí uilechumhachtaigh, dearc anuas ar do sheirbhísigh A. agus A. atá aontaithe sa phósadh anseo inniu, agus tabhair dóibh, as ucht a ngrá dá chéile, go mairfidh a ngrá duitse go buan.
Sin é ár nguí chugat trí Chríost ár dTiarna.

P: Amen.